Pre-release comments about *Badass*

"Kathy Sierra wants you to understand this: If your users like themselves better when they use what you make, they'll recommend it with a fervor money simply cannot buy. No one gets this more clearly than Sierra, and *Badass* is her way of helping you get it too."

Clay Shirky
Author of *Here Comes Everybody* and *Cognitive Surplus*

"In *Badass*, Kathy Sierra—one of our brightest business minds -- offers up a surprising insight into what makes certain offerings shine in a competitive marketplace. Believe it or not, many people don't care how awesome your product is. Instead, they care about how awesome they are when they use your product. If you can tap into that motivation, you've got gold. This books shows you how."

Daniel H. Pink
Author of New York Times bestsellers *To Sell is Human* and *Drive*

"Do NOT let the breezy presentation of the ideas here convince you that the ideas themselves are lightweight. They're not. Kathy Sierra has become an expert in where expertise comes from, and with in this book she'll show you how to make your product's users experts. Or, as she puts it, badass, which is the perfect label for Kathy and for this book."

Andrew McAfee
Cofounder of MIT's Initiative on the Digital Economy and coauthor of *The Second Machine Age*

"Every once in a while, someone comes along who sees the world more clearly, and helps you to do the same. Every time I read Kathy Sierra, or hear her speak, I feel smarter, more thoughtful, and more caring. She has that gift of making everyone around her better. But what's even more special, the "better" she helps you with is the ability to help other people get better! Genius!"

Tim O'Reilly
Founder and CEO of O'Reilly Media

Badass

Making Users Awesome

Kathy Sierra

Beijing · Cambridge · Farnham · Köln · Sebastopol · Tokyo

Badass: Making Users Awesome

by Kathy Sierra

Copyright © 2015 Kathy Sierra. All rights reserved.

Printed in Canada.

Published by O'Reilly Media, Inc., 1005 Gravenstein Highway North, Sebastopol, CA 95472.

O'Reilly books may be purchased for educational, business, or sales promotional use. Online editions are also available for most titles (*http://safaribooksonline.com*). For more information, contact our corporate/institutional sales department: 800-998-9938 or corporate@oreilly.com.

Editors: Courtney Nash, Mike Loukides, and Meghan Blanchette	**Interior Designer:** Kathy Sierra
	Cover Designer: Edie Freedman
Copyeditor: Octal Publishing, Inc.	**Illustrator:** Kathy Sierra

February 2015:   First Edition

Revision History for the First Edition
2015-01-23:   First Release
2015-03-06:   Second Release

See *http://oreilly.com/catalog/errata.csp?isbn=9781491919019* for release details.

978-1-491-91901-9

[TI]

Badass: Making Users Awesome

> This product **must** be a bestseller. *Or else.*

The Challenge

Prologue

> *How does he do that? Perfect every time.*

What Experts Do

> *They said it would be easy. This can't be right...*

Help Them Move Forward

> I never thought I'd be able to do this. It's amazing.

Support Cognitive Resources

The Challenge
▼
Prologue

Imagine this happened to you

> You **must** make a bestseller. *Or else.*

Imagine someone *forced* you to create a new bestselling product or service.

What would you do?

> Oh, and don't count on a
> big marketing budget.
> No PR media tour.
> No fancy launch party.

One more thing...

> You can't simply be the lowest-priced. This has to be about sustainable success.

The clock is ticking. Everything depends on whether you can make a *sustainable* bestselling product or service.

Where do you start?
What questions do you ask yourself?

> Given competing equally-priced, equally-promoted products , why **are** some products far more successful than others?

What's different about the bestsellers?

Why did these sell...

...but those didn't?

Sustained bestsellers   NOT successful

Our search for a formula begins with a question: why do *these* keep selling but *those* don't? What attributes do the bestsellers have that their competitors don't?

If we can't use marketing and lowest price, what *else* could fuel the success of bestselling products and services?

Something they *do*?
Something they *are*?
Something they *have*?

> *Maybe we can reverse-engineer successful products and services to find what they have in common.*

We need to find common attributes across products and services that are *sustainably* successful. There must be *something* we can use to make a formula...

What's our big fear?

> *It can't just be luck, right? Because if it really all comes down to luck...*

Luck always plays a role

Our job is to shrink the role luck plays.

We don't have the luxury of rolling the dice and crossing our fingers. We must increase our odds.

*When it's **not** luck or marketing or lowest price... what is it?*

Does the *best* product win?
Does desirability increase as a function of quality?

Desirability

Quality

We use "desirability" here to include not only what we *want-but-don't-have*, but also what we *have*-and-*want-to-keep/replace*.

When you remove luck, marketing, and price from the equation, is it *quality* that drives desirability?

Is it simply **best** product wins?

And if it's *quality* that drives desirability, *who* defines "quality" and "best" for a particular product or service? Is it based on objective measurements of craftsmanship and materials? Is it about speed or durability? Beauty? Strength? User-friendliness? How does our definition of quality shift depending on the product type and market demographics?

No, there are too many examples where "best" is not the bestseller...

<u>This</u> is also true

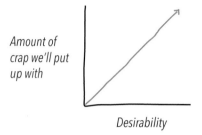

Amount of crap we'll put up with

Desirability

Tolerance for problems is a function of desirability

Even if we *could* define "quality" in some useful, objective way for a given product or service, if we *really* like something, we're willing to accept flaws, problems, issues, even a higher price.

Quality can drive desirability.
Desirability can drive (perceived) quality.

*And high desirability makes us willing to do more than just **tolerate** flaws...*

And this is also true

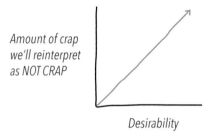

Amount of crap we'll reinterpret as NOT CRAP

Desirability

*Reframing problems as **not**-problems is a function of desirability*

Desirability changes our perception of "flaws." The more we love something, the more likely we are to not just *tolerate* problems but reinterpret them as *not* problems.

We minimize, downplay, deny.
We spin bugs as features.

Product/service love is (nearly) blind.

For our formula, we'll have to look somewhere else. *Quality* (whatever that actually means) doesn't guarantee *desirability*.

> If **highest quality** isn't our answer, where else can we look? If the goal is **desirability**, what makes that happen?

None of this matters if nobody knows about us. We need marketing!

Just because we don't have a marketing *budget* doesn't mean we're not *doing marketing*. But when we look at sustainably successful products and services, the common attribute is *not* their marketing.

We can all name high-profile massive marketing failures (think: Windows 8).

But our challenge explicitly rules out a big marketing *budget*. Out-spending the competition on marketing is not an option, but what's the alternative?

Let's ask some "friends"...

Here's what my "friends" and social media consultants say:

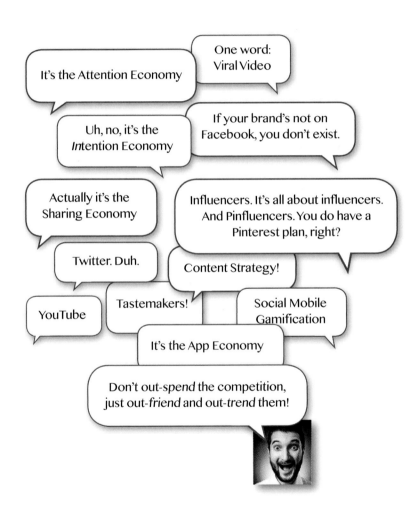

It's the Attention Economy

One word: Viral Video

Uh, no, it's the *In*tention Economy

If your brand's not on Facebook, you don't exist.

Actually it's the Sharing Economy

Influencers. It's all about influencers. And Pinfluencers. You do have a Pinterest plan, right?

Twitter. Duh.

Content Strategy!

YouTube

Tastemakers!

Social Mobile Gamification

It's the App Economy

Don't out-*spend* the competition, just out-*friend* and out-*trend* them!

A strategy based on out-friend or out-trend the competition is exhausting and fragile.

What does an out-friend/out-trend strategy hope to "win"?

The brand engagement arms race.

They're on Pinterest? We need to be there. They've got YouTube videos? Let's do that too. And oh, look, yet *another* new social network where our brand needs a "presence."

Trying to stay one *follower*, one *like*, one *meme*, ahead of competitors is *not* a robust, durable strategy. It is *not* a sustainable path to long-term success.

And is "engagement" *really* what we want?

And when you grow up, you'll get to **engage** with **brands**!

If it drains *our* energy to out-engage our competitors, imagine what all this brand engagement does to our *users*?

On their deathbed, nobody will say:

"If only I'd engaged more with brands."

If we can't out-*spend*, out-*friend*, or out-*trend* the competition, how *else* can we build desirability?

Which brings us back to... *how?*

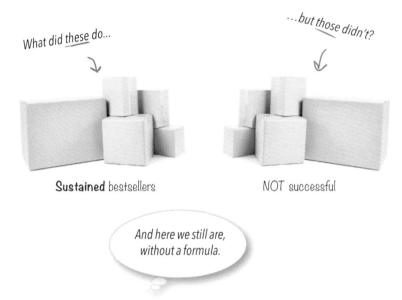

What did <u>these</u> do...

...but <u>those</u> didn't?

Sustained bestsellers

NOT successful

And here we still are,
without a formula.

If we can't out-spend, out-friend, or out-trend the competition, what's left?

What *does* make a difference? What *are* the attributes of the long-term bestsellers?

This. *The bestsellers had this:*

Every moment of every day, somebody mentions something they *love-could-not-do-without.* Whether face-to-face or in blogs, reviews, discussions, tweets, comments, updates, texts, photos—people *talk.*

Sustained bestsellers are recommended.

And it makes all the difference.

In this book we mean "recommended" *literally.* When we say *word of mouth (WOM)* think *only* of honest, *nonincentivized* comments about either the product or the results the user got with it.

When people talk about a brand's contest to win an iPad, or a funny viral video, they're talking about the brand's *marketing,* and that's *not* the word of mouth we're looking for.

Word of Mouth

92% *say they trust*
recommendations from friends and family above all other forms of advertising

70% *say they trust online*
consumer reviews, the second most trusted recommendation above all other forms of advertising.

Source: Nielsen's Global Trust in Advertising report
http://www.nielsen.com/us/en/reports/2012/global-trust-in-advertising-and-brand-messages.html

The answer begins here.
True, *trusted* recommendations.

Not faked, bribed, or bought.

Not a *brand* masquerading as our *"friend"* on social media.

It doesn't have to be from a person we actually know in real-life, but it must be from someone (or something) we trust *more* than we trust a brand. And most of us still trust a total stranger on Amazon more than the "brand friend" we "like" on Facebook. (That we "liked" for a chance to win an iPod.)

Note: Amazon reviews aren't entirely trusted either, thanks to well-publicized stories of fake positive reviews by the author or fake negative reviews by a rival. *Even in the face of potentially fake reviews, we still trust them more than we trust the brand's own messages.*

The Challenge
▼
Prologue

We're still left with the Big Question: If it's honest word of mouth that drives sustained success, what drives word of mouth?

Why do users recommend these...

...but not those?

Sustained bestsellers

NOT successful

If the common attribute of sustained bestsellers is "recommended by trusted sources," the real question is: **what inspires those recommendations?**

First, a pop quiz:

Which would you rather have a user *feel*?
Which of these would be a better predictor of sustained success?
Which of these feelings inspires more honest word of mouth?

*Imagine you were forced to pick just one**

A

B

C

*Yes, "it depends" but think of it as, "In general, this one would probably be the best reflection of success."

It's Secret Answer D

(Sorry, this was a trick question.)

I'm awesome!

It's not about our *product*, our *company*, our *brand*.

It's not about how the user feels about *us*.

It's about how the user feels about *himself*, in the context of whatever it is our product, service, cause helps him do and be.

> But people don't actually talk like that. Nobody says, "I'm awesome" because of a product. They say, "I love this" or "This app is amazing."

It's not about the actual *words* they say, but about the *feelings* that inspired them to say it. "*I'm* awesome because of this" is the *feeling* behind their actual words, "This *thing* is awesome".

They don't say they like the product because they like _the product._

They say they like the product because they like _themselves._

What he **says:**   What he **means:**

This **product** is amazing. You should see what **it** does...

I am amazing. You should see what **I** **can do** with it...

Word of mouth as a key to our formula. We want people to say, "You **must** get this!"

But behind their authentic recommendation is a feeling about what this product enabled them to do or be.

We've been looking in the wrong place

The key attributes of sustained success don't live in the *product*.

The key attributes live in the user.

Instead of looking for common attributes across successful *products*, we must look for common attributes across successful *users* of those products.

"Awesome product!" is a side-effect

What we
THINK is true

What's
ACTUALLY
true

Our users don't bask in the glow of
our awesome product.

Our product basks in the glow of
our users' result with it.

Exercise: write your ideal Amazon review

Don't turn the page until you've at least thought about it.

This is not a *marketing* exercise on the reviews or testimonials most likely to drive sales. This is about reviews that best reflect what we hope our users will think and feel.

Do this exercise *without* thinking about how good the review makes your product/brand look to others.

☆☆☆☆☆   *Write your review here*

Which of these do you prefer?

 Wonderful product! I love it!

This is an excellent product! Easy to use, yet powerful. Looks like it will last forever. You won't regret this purchase!

Looks good, but reads like a brochure.
It's mostly about the **product**.

 Amazing! Works perfectly!

The instructions were a little weak, but I was able to set it up myself in less than 5 minutes. I've already made amazing progress with it in three weeks! You won't regret this purchase!

Much better! Reviewer talks about **herself** and her **results**.

We want to build products, service, and support in ways that inspire users to talk about *themselves*.

But there's a problem...

A sad Venn diagram

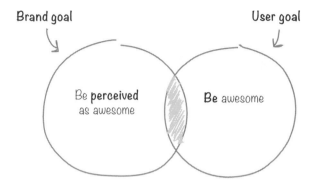

Brand goal

User goal

Be perceived as awesome

Be awesome

Too often, the goals of a company and the goals of its users aren't just *different* but *mutually exclusive*.

How do we move from THIS...

...to THIS?

Brand goal   User goal

Brand goal   User goal

If the answer lives not in the *product* but in the successful *user*, what are the common attributes of a successful user?

What does it mean to be a "successful" user?

The Challenge
▼
Prologue

Reverse-engineering Successful Users

If we look at successful users across a wide range of products, services, hobbies, etc. we find common attributes. The first step in *creating* successful users is to *observe* successful users.

How do they behave? What do they do? What do they say?

At the core, though, there's **one** key attribute of successful users that's driving all of the others. What is it?

Where you find successful users, you find users that are...

Successful users means badass users

Not badass *products*, badass *users*.

Not amazing *apps*, amazing *users*.

Where you find *sustained* success driven by recommendations, you find *badass users*. Smarter, more skillful, more powerful users. Users who *know* more and can *do* more in a way that's personally meaningful.

*Users don't evangelize to their friends because they like the **product**, they evangelize to their friends because they like their **friends**.* (inspired by a quote from Mike Arauz)

The bar is lower for competing on *user* awesomeness vs. *product* awesomeness

Most companies compete on the quality of the product, not the quality of the user's results with the product. Competing on user awesome means fewer direct competitors, even within the same product/service category.

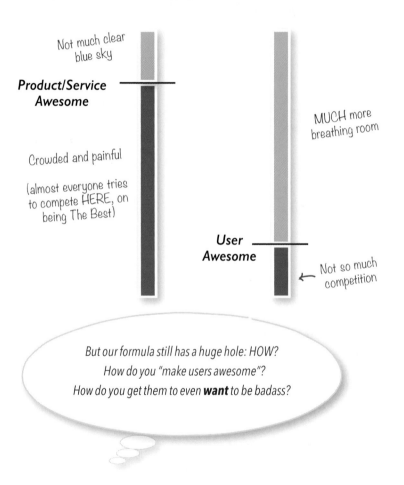

(Note: this graph was inspired in part by W. Chan Kim and Renée Mauborgne's "Blue Ocean Strategy.")

What do these have in common?

Colors on my latest video came out perfect.

I built this in less than two hours.

They said I got the deal because of those charts in my spreadsheet.

The Challenge
▼
Prologue

Results

User **Badass** = User **Results**
Badass users are **better** users.
Much better.

It's about what they can *do* or *be*
as a result of what our product,
service, experience *enables*.

Sustained bestsellers help their
users get badass *results*.

*Yeah, just one small thing...
badass at WHAT? What about simple utilities?
What if there's nothing to be badass at?*

*Before we can create badass
users, we must answer the
question, "Badass at what?"*

Badass at... *what?*

What happens if we don't make snowboards, video editing software, or anything else that someone *can* become badass at?

Imagine a tiny little utility tool "X."

What does having X *enable?*

What can people *now* do because of X that they *couldn't* do without it?

What can people now do *better* because of X?

What are people *not* doing now but *could* if they took advantage of all that X supports?

That's just a warm-up. The exercise on the next set of pages will ask you to define something linked to your product, service, or cause that users *can* become badass at. Regardless of how unlikely it may seem, _anything_ can be linked to the potential for badass results. The key lies in answering this:

"What are you a *subset* of?"

Even if you already know what badass means for your product or service, don't skip this quick exercise. We'll refer to pieces of it throughout the rest of the book, and it might give you more ideas for *new* things your users *can* become badass at.

The Superset Exercise

(Answering "Badass at *what?*")

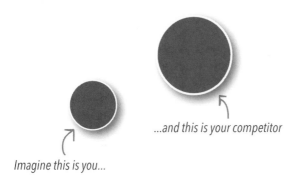

...and this is your competitor

Imagine this is you...

Or maybe your relative sizes are reversed:

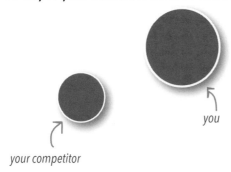

you

your competitor

But how big you are relative to your competition is not what matters here.

What matters most is asking one crucial question...

What are you both a *subset* of?

Your thing is a subset of some bigger, more *compelling* thing.
What's the context in which your product or service is used?

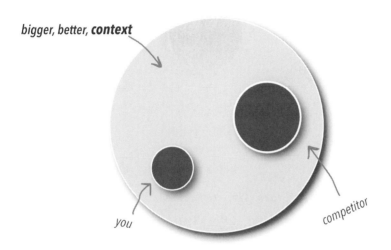

bigger, better, **context**

you

competitor

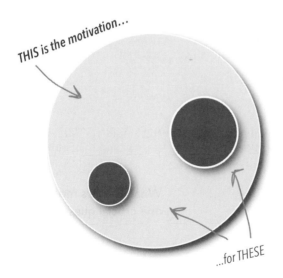

THIS is the motivation...

...for THESE

What's your bigger compelling context?

What are you a *subset* of?

(You could have many different answers,
depending on how far you expand the context.)

Example

bigger, compelling **context**

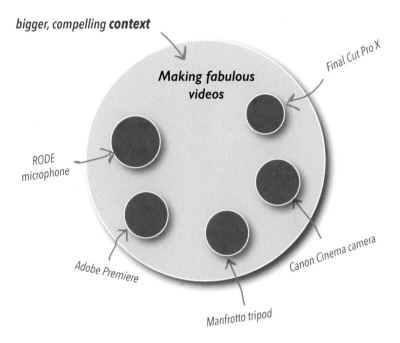

Video editing software, cameras, lighting, and microphones
are all *subsets* of video creation.

Nobody says this.

Most products and services support a bigger, compelling, motivating context.

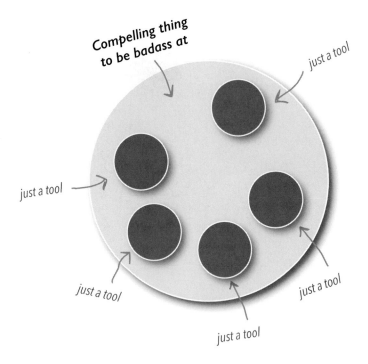

Tools *matter*. But being a *master of the tool* is rarely our user's ultimate goal. Most tools (products, services) *enable and support* the user's true–*and more motivating*–goal.

Nobody wants to be a *tripod master*. We want to *use* tripods to make amazing videos.

More Superset Examples

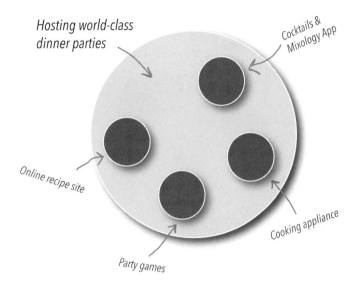

Hosting world-class dinner parties

Cocktails & Mixology App

Online recipe site

Cooking appliance

Party games

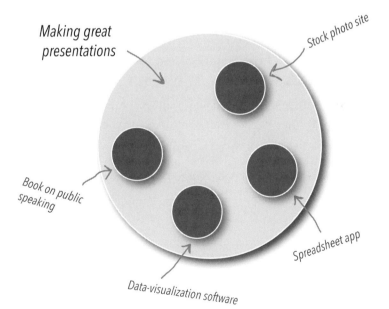

Making great presentations

Stock photo site

Book on public speaking

Spreadsheet app

Data-visualization software

Contexts all the way out

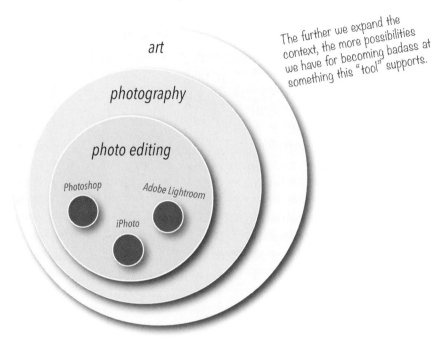

art

photography

photo editing

Photoshop

Adobe Lightroom

iPhoto

The further we expand the context, the more possibilities we have for becoming badass at something this "tool" supports.

People don't want to be badass at using our tool.
They want be badass at what our tool helps them do.

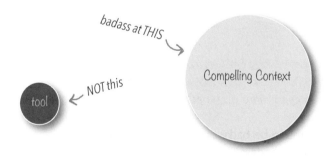

badass at THIS

NOT this

tool

Compelling Context

What's wrong here?

Before *they give us money*   **After** *they give us money*

Photography   Camera

Compelling Context

tool

Good marketing focuses on what the potential user *really* wants to do. But *after* they buy? Every experience the user has with us shifts to *just the tool*.

Think about this.

If we want sustained, committed, badass users, we must fix this. *After* they give us money or join our service we should focus even *more* on what they really want to do.

The don't want to be badass at our *thing*.
They want to be badass at what they *do* with it.
They want badass *results*.

Not cameras... *photography*

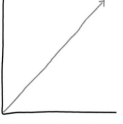

Appreciation for higher-end versions, add-ons, upgrades, etc.

Photography Skills

Some people have a passion for *cameras*, but most of us don't buy a camera to get a *camera*. We buy it to take *photos*.

And the deeper we get into *photography*, the more likely we are to recognize and appreciate the benefits of higher-end *cameras*.

In other words, it's the *context*—not the tool—that builds desirability for more/better tools.

Being better is Better

Being better means better *results*.

But being better is about more than just *results*. Being more skillful, more knowledgeable, more advanced is itself an intrinsically rewarding experience. The ability to make finer distinctions in what you can see, hear, taste, perceive in the environment can feel like a superpower.

When you're more skilled at something, it's as though a part of your world got an upgrade. It's as though *pre*-badass-you had been experiencing the world in *Standard* and now a part of the world has become **High Resolution.**

Badass is about more than just *results*

Badass means higher resolution.
Badass means deeper, richer experiences.

classical music expert "hears" more in the music than most of us

The *better* you get at [x], the more *detail* you perceive in [x]. Greater detail is one of the most overlooked benefits of being better. To the human (and animal) brain, the ability to "pick-up" more from the environment is deeply rewarding.

While the ability to gain more resolution in *music* is an obvious benefit, having a higher-res experience of nearly *anything* makes that experience more pleasurable.

High-res is like a superpower

The wine sommelier smells and tastes more than most of us.

While most people see stars as the lights in the night sky, an astronomer sees a rich pattern of named stars and constellations.

To those who don't know chess, it's just pieces arbitrarily placed on the board, but to a strong chess player, a glance at a good game in progress is filled with tension and intrigue.

(Side-effect: a good chess player watching a movie will notice if the chess game in the scene shows a "real" game, and they notice when the pieces aren't in the same place between shots.)

The Challenge
▼
Prologue

Higher *resolution* means higher-end *products*

The *better* you get at [x], the more *distinctions* you perceive in [x]. Enhanced perception means the ability to appreciate the value of higher-end and/or more advanced versions of products. An audiophile, for example, might perceive a substantial difference between two speaker systems, while a non-audiophile swears the speakers are identical.

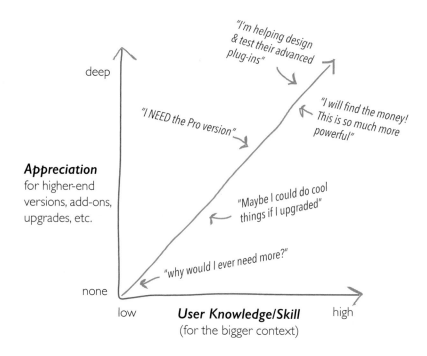

Don't just upgrade your *product*, upgrade your *users*.

Another benefit of badass:
Badass users won't shut up

Badass users *talk.* They're our best source of authentic, unincentivized word of mouth. The word of mouth our "formula" depends on.

But there's something even better than word of mouth...

**We want them to talk, but if they're badass...
they might not need to**

Did you see Roy's latest video? The color is amazing.

He said he used a new film-look app. I want it!

Badass users talk. They can't help it.
But sometimes they don't need to *talk* about their amazing capabilities and results.

Sometimes it's *obvious*.

Word OF Obvious (WOFO)
is even better than
Word Of Mouth (WoM)

More *badass* means more *business*

We want word of mouth and word of obvious. We want our users to become better and better at the bigger context, and help encourage others to do the same.

How did you get that creamy, out-of-focus background? My camera can't do this.

Go to the Canon website and learn about aperture and depth of field.

Looks like I'll need a new camera and lens to do this.

But beware of faux-badass

Gamification awards for purchases, visits to a website, comments, etc. typically reward behavior the company wants, not what the user wants.

It's not about helping people *feel* badass. It's about helping them *be* badass.

Have they gained new *higher resolution* at the bigger context they care about?

Are they now *more skilled* at the bigger context they care about?

Do they now *know more,* and can they use their new knowledge in ways they find useful or meaningful?

Are they getting better results?

Competing on *Customer Service* Excellence doesn't necessarily mean *User* Excellence

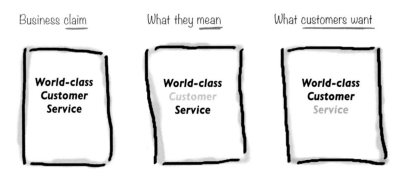

Business claim | What they mean | What customers want

World-class Customer Service | World-class Customer Service | World-class Customer Service

"Fabulous Customer Service" *sounds* user-centered but it's often just a company-centered focus *masquerading* as user-centered. No matter how pampered our users feel, if it doesn't help them grow their skills, resolution, and results, it's still *faux* badass. The role of customer service is to support and enable users to not just *feel* better, but to *be* better. Service plays a big role, but it's not the star.

Competing on out-*caring* the competition is fragile unless "caring" means "caring about user results."

Always be thinking: **They're people not puppies**

"Feeling loved by a brand" does not mean badass. If we love *our* users more than the competition loves *theirs*, the proof doesn't live in what *we* do, but in what *our users* do as a result.

The *Better User* POV:

Don't just make a better [X], make a better User of [X]

Don't make a better [*camera*],
make a better [*photographer*]

Don't make a better [*power drill*],
make a better [*home DIY builder*]

Don't make a better [*our service*],
make a better [*user of our service*]

Your turn:

your X

Don't make a better [_____], make a better [_____]

your users (in the bigger context)

(You might have many different versions of this for different uses
and/or market segments. If you're still figuring out your bigger
context—the thing you'll help users become excellent at—then just
pick *something* for now.)

Where we're at now:

Sustained *desirability drives success.*

Honest, non-bribed *word of mouth drives desirability.*

User badass drives word of mouth.

Badass not at the *tool*, but at what the tool *enables.*

Badass at the *bigger context.*

Badass means *higher resolution.*

Badass means *user results.*

(But not *faux* badass)

Don't make a better [x], make a better [user of X].

And yet we STILL haven't answered the REAL question...

Which brings us yet again to... *how?*

How did <u>these</u> make badass users?

Sustained bestsellers   NOT successful

How do you *make* users badass?
How do you help them *want* to be badass?
How do you get them to be users *before* they're badass?

We're almost there.

The Challenge

▼

Prologue ▶**Think Badass**

"Point of view is worth 80 IQ points"

— Alan Kay

Point of view is also worth a big marketing budget, a pile of social media *Likes*, or a viral video.

Our POV:

To create sustained success, create high-resolution, badass users.

Design for the Post-UX UX

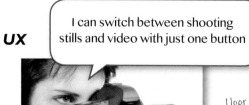

UX

I can switch between shooting stills and video with just one button

User Experience while using the "tool"

Post-UX UX

Wow. The comments on my video are inspiring.

User Experience after using the "tool".

The UX of **results**.

All that matters is what happens when the clicking's done

When *our* results are tied to the results of our *users*, all that matters is what happens when the clicking, swiping, interacting, using is *done*.

What did that experience **enable**?

What can they now **do**?

What can they now **show others**?

What will they **say** to others?

How are they now more **powerful**?

What happens *after* the UX drives our success. It's what drives our users to talk about and recommend us, and it's what leaves our users so obviously better that they might not *need* to.

Thought Experiment: *Post-UX documentary*

Imagine one of your users gave a documentary camera crew full access to track them *after* they use your product or service.

What do they do in the next minutes, hours, days, weeks?

Who do they talk to? What do they say?

If a documentary crew followed one of your users, what would the camera see and hear?

They leave your site, store, or app. They put down your tool. What happens *now*?

Write a detailed description of what you see and hear, for the time-frame that makes sense for your bigger context.

You can do variations of this exercise for users at different levels from first-time newbie to expert. The key is to start thinking—**hard**—about what most products and services don't: the *post*-UX UX.

Thought Experiment: *User at a Dinner Party*

How do you help your user be more interesting at a dinner party?

Designing for the post-UX UX means designing not just for *your* users but for your *users'* users.

It's not so much what our user thinks of *us* but what our user's friends, family, peers think of *our user*.

Imagine one of your users at a dinner party, and describe what you do (or *could* do) to help him be more interesting at that party. What have you given him to *talk* about (that isn't about *you*). What have you given him to *show*?

Thought Experiment: *Search And Replace*

Imagine you're in a meeting brainstorming brand perception, and marketing. Now imagine that instead of asking questions about *your* brand, you try replacing "our" with "our *users*." It won't always make sense at first, but act as if it *does*.

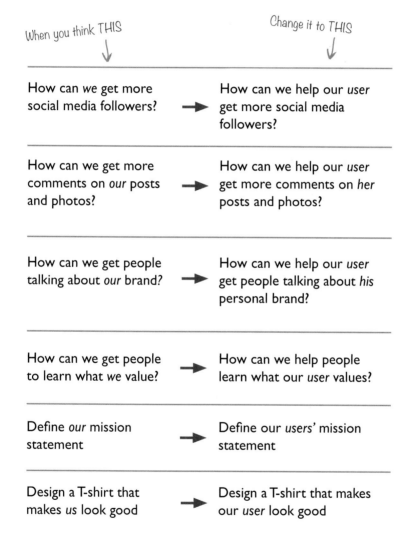

When you think THIS

Change it to THIS

How can *we* get more social media followers?	How can we help our *user* get more social media followers?
How can we get more comments on *our* posts and photos?	How can we help our *user* get more comments on *her* posts and photos?
How can we get people talking about *our* brand?	How can we help our *user* get people talking about *his* personal brand?
How can we get people to learn what *we* value?	How can we help people learn what our *user* values?
Define *our* mission statement	Define our *users'* mission statement
Design a T-shirt that makes *us* look good	Design a T-shirt that makes our *user* look good

Thought Experiment: *your* users competing against *their* users

*"**Our** users are better at this than **their** users"*

Imagine that your competitive advantage is not how *you* compare to the competition but how your *users* compare to the competition's users.

Imagine, for example, that instead of marketing based on *your* benchmarks, your marketing showed your *users'* benchmarks.

Describe or sketch an imaginary ad that shows your users out-performing your competition's users at the bigger context:

> *Yes, we get it. User badass. Our users beat their users,*
> *etc.etc.etc. But this "formula" means nothing if*
> **nobody knows about you.**

Somebody has to be the first user. If our product or service is new, the goal is the same: create badass users. It *does* mean putting energy into getting at least a few initial users who are likely to become better *and* are in a context where others will know about it.

This does *not* mean getting an "influencer" to promote the new thing. Remember the search-and-replace exercise? Instead of asking "where do we *find* an influencer?" ask "how can we *create* an influencer from a person who is active in our target audience and most likely to benefit from becoming better?"

Later in the book we'll look at techniques for helping those first users *recognize* they're getting better, as early as possible, and increase the chance that others in the target audience will *hear about it.*

The best place to begin is to help a few people become *noticeably* better at the bigger context, and let word of mouth and word of *obvious* emerge as natural side effects.

The Challenge

▼

Prologue ►Think Badass ►**The User Journey**

The Badass User Curve

Remember: it's about the bigger context.

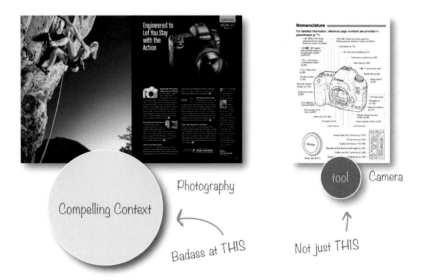

Photography

Compelling Context

tool Camera

Badass at THIS

Not just THIS

If your tool is complex, with its *own* challenging expertise curve, you might have *one* learning curve with key milestones for using your *tool*, and a different curve and milestones for the *compelling context*.

If you haven't yet defined your compelling context, make one up as a placeholder to use for the rest of the book.

The User Curve

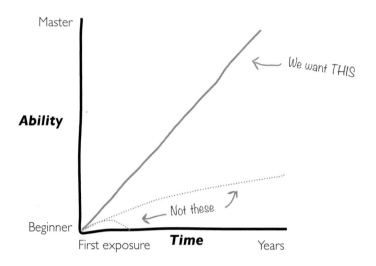

The goal: **up and to the right**

She who gets her users further and faster up the curve has a better chance for success.

Our company might have *two* curves to care about—one for our product ("*tool*") and one for the bigger *context* in which it's used. If our product is quick and easy to master, we can focus exclusively on helping users with the compelling context curve. But if our tool *is* complex or difficult with a potentially long learning and mastery curve, we'll need to think about where our users are on *both* curves.

What is your user curve like today?

Example: fictional entry-level camera maker:

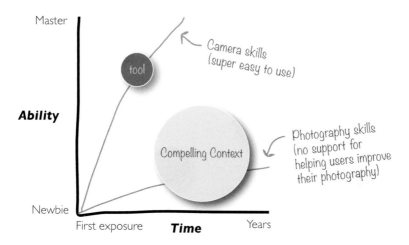

Imagine a camera maker that markets inexpensive point-and-shoot cameras. The company nailed the usability, and developed an excellent user guide and online video tutorials.

Their motto is: "user must be taking pictures within 12 minutes" and everything the company does is focused on that goal. New users go from unboxing to taking pictures immediately. Their users move up the camera (tool) curve more quickly than their competitors' users.

But the company does *nothing* to help users advance their *photography* skills. Their users have no new abilities and results to show off or talk about.

Draw your current user curves

For your *product/service*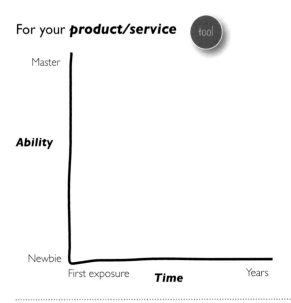

For the *compelling context*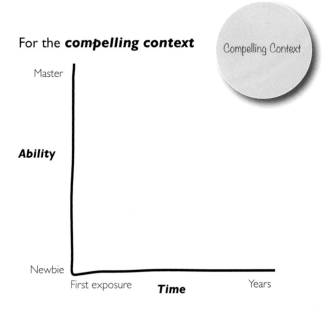

Key Thresholds

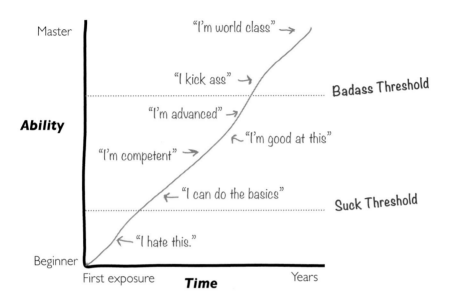

The ideal curve continues **up and to the right.** Users don't drop out or plateau. They keep going. They keep making progress. *They keep getting better.*

Along the way they'll hit many milestones, some more crucial than others. But of all points on the curve, the two most important are *crossing the Suck Threshold* and *crossing the Badass Threshold.*

Later we'll look at strategies for helping our users push through these thresholds to keep moving forward.

Danger in the Suck Zone

The most vulnerable time for new users is in The Suck Zone. If
we lose them here, we won't get them back. (Later we'll look
at ways to help them through it.)

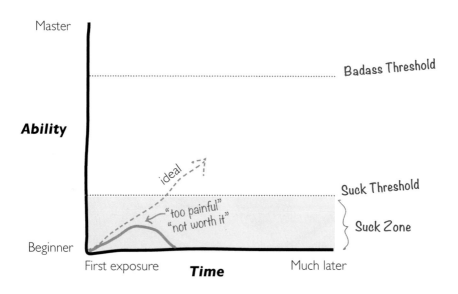

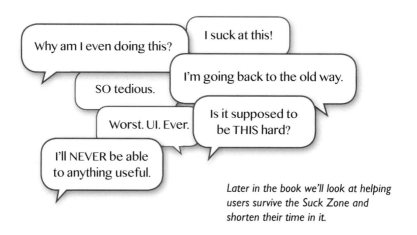

*Later in the book we'll look at helping
users survive the Suck Zone and
shorten their time in it.*

Why they don't upgrade (or switch brands)

Nobody wants to go *back* to the Suck Zone

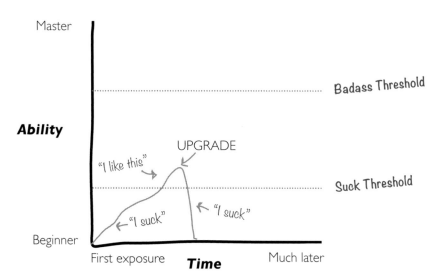

Your users clawed their way over the Suck Threshold. *Finally* they can *do* something. They're competent.

Along comes the NEW AWESOME IMPROVED version. "Upgrade!" we said. "You'll love it!" we said.

And just like that, they're back in the Suck Zone. Whether it's a new version of a product or a new process, change is most painful when we *lose previously hard-fought ability.* It now takes *more* effort and frustration to do what we used to do.

Returning to the Suck Zone rarely seems worth it, despite promises that the upgrade will makes us more powerful.

Crossing the Suck Threshold and leveling off

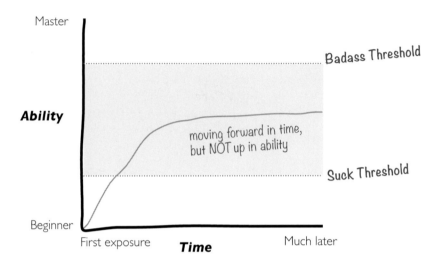

They crossed the Suck Threshold and moved firmly into intermediate range. *And stayed.* They're still your user. This might look good on a spreadsheet for user retention.

But if they're no longer moving up and to the right, they aren't increasing resolution, gaining new skills, or becoming more powerful. Their enthusiasm for their new abilities and results will slowly fade.

The benefits of badass depend on users steadily moving up the curve, not leveling off at "competent." Consistent, competent users who level off might be reasonably happy and comfortably loyal, but for our sustainable bestseller, *comfortably competent* might not be enough. We need those dinner party conversations.

The Stuck Zone looks good, but isn't

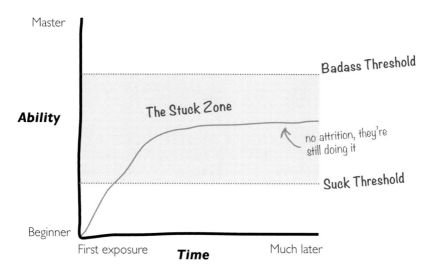

Every day, someone unpacks their first digital SLR camera with full manual control over shutter speed, aperture, and ISO. But even the most powerful cameras usually come with one or more "easy modes," so they set the dial on **AUTO** and click away.

And there they stay. They *want* to do more, but if they start experimenting with manual exposure they might take *unusable* photos. With great new manual *power* comes great *potential for backsliding to the Suck Zone.*

Auto mode is seductive. It's easy, comfortable, safe. But if our users don't break free, they might never develop a deeper interest in photography. If they don't push past the Stuck Zone, they aren't *painting with light,* they're just... *taking snapshots.*

Where do your users get stuck?

What's the equivalent of AUTO mode for your users?

What's the AUTO mode for *your* product, service, bigger cooler context? What is it that holds people in the competent zone but keeps them from pushing forward? What are the comfort-able-but-limiting tools and techniques they use that they must leave behind to make progress?

List the ways in which your users get stuck, at both your tool (if relevant) and at the compelling context:

What if entry-level/beginner tools are all we offer?

> *A great photographer can be amazing with just a camera phone. And what about the company that makes ONLY entry-level point-and-shoot cameras?*

If the tool you make does *not* support advanced skills within the compelling context you've chosen, what do you do? Some companies grow with their users and eventually develop more advanced versions of their tool(s). But that's not always an option.

Imagine you're the point-and-shoot camera maker without any higher-end gear in your future plans. Will your users outgrow you as you help them become better? Will they outgrow you even faster *because* you helped them become better?

Entry-level *products* don't have to mean entry-level *context*.

An entry-level camera maker can help users become badass at the subset of photography skills that *don't* depend on manual controls. Instead of helping them master full exposure control with shutter speed and aperture, what about gear-independent artistic and technical skills like composition and lighting?

If you make *only* entry-level tools, think about the context subset you *can* enable

DSLR camera	Point & Shoot camera
Photography Context	Photography Context

Manual exposure	Manual exposure
Color manipulation	Color manipulation
Manual focus	Manual focus
Depth of field	Depth of field
Portraits	Portraits
Sports photography	Sports photography
Nature photography	Nature photography
Black & White	Black & White
Fine art	Fine art
Digital editing	Digital editing
Composition	Composition
Lighting	Lighting

Can help users with any/ all aspects of photography

focus here

What if my users don't want to be a total badass? What if they just want to be reasonably good at it?

And that whole path-to-master is intimidating and feels like overkill when they're thinking, "Hey, I just want to get something DONE, not be a ninja."

We don't have to make our users the Chuck Norris of our context

For WOM and WOFO, we DON'T need THAT...   THIS will do

Our users don't have to go *all the way to world-class* to experience the intrinsic rewards of high resolution knowledge, skills, and results.

Simply getting past the Suck Zone can feel badass.

In many challenging domains, just going from zero to *any* capability is motivating.

People first learning computer programming often start by writing code that prints "Hello World" to the screen. That's it. Just "Hello World." But if you've never written a line of code before, seeing "Hello World" on the display can seem like a superpower.

> *You didn't answer the question. Why should they work on being badass if they don't want to actually be badass?*

Just for clarity: let's assume we're talking about users who *do* want to be *better* but *don't* want to go all the way to Chuck Norris of X. (Not *yet* anyway.) If they don't want to be better *at all*, that's a different issue, and one we won't spend time worrying about.

We *assume* that at least *some* initial motivation—a desire to become better at the bigger context—*is already there*. While the *initial* spark of motivation is rarely a problem, the big challenge is helping that tiny spark become a sustainable flame.

By treating users as if they *were* trying to be badass, we help *all* users build higher resolution abilities. We don't create a separate "good but not expert" path. *It's all one path, and some go further than others.*

If you're worried users will be intimidated by a path-to-badass when they "just want to be good enough to get something done," the solution is simple: just *tell* them. Let *them* know that the early steps are the same no matter how far up the expertise curve they want to go.

(We'll look at motivation much more deeply later in the book.)

Things change when you start to improve

Day **1**:

I **just** want to have **fun** on the slopes and not die. It's not like I'm **ever** gonna do the back-country...

You say that NOW, but wait 'till your first powder day.

Day **20**:

So...what *does* it take to be good enough to do the back-country? Asking for a friend.

Told you.

And here we are STILL without a formula.
We know **what** to do, but... **_how_**? How,
exactly, do we help users become badass?

What Experts Do
▼
Science of Badass

Moving up and to the right

How do we help our users keep moving up and to the right on the user journey? We must do at least *two* things: help them continue *building* skills/resolution/abilities, and help them continue *wanting* to.

It all begins with understanding the science of badass, but remember: this is about getting better at not just our tool, but at the compelling context in which they will (or could) use it.

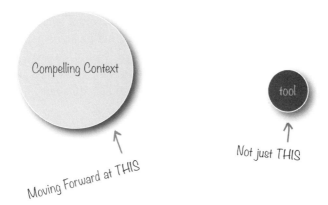

Science of Badass = Science of Expertise

We won't find much academic research on becoming *badass*. But there *is* a robust, practical, science of expert performance and the development of expertise. In addition to the "formal" science of expertise, many other areas of scientific research give us tools and techniques for knowledge and skill acquisition.

From this point forward in the book we'll use "badass," "expertise," "expert performance," and "mastery" interchangeably. People often use "expert" to mean *well-known* in a domain, regardless of *measurable* performance. But in the science of expertise, the word "expert" has a more precise definition based on demonstrated ability and results.

Expertise is not about popularity, or years of experience, or even depth of knowledge.

Experts are not what they know but what they do.
Repeatedly.

The science of expertise applies to *everything*

Whether it's dancing, brain surgery, guitar, cooking, chess, archery, or engineering, where we find deep expertise we find common attributes for how that expertise was built. Technical, creative, intuitive, logical, analytical, physical, mental, emotional—the science of expertise applies to *any* domain.

Before we can help our users become badass, we must define what expertise is for our bigger context. What does it mean to be expert at using our tool within the bigger context? What does it look like? What are expert *results*?

Technical definition of badass

*Given a **representative** task in the domain, a badass performs in a **superior** way, more **reliably**.*

Experts are what they *do*.

It's not just what they *know*.
It's what they *do* with what they know.
And it's their ability to do it *again* and *again* and *again*.

Expert/badass performance is both *superior* and *more consistent* than the performance of those who are knowledgeable and experienced but *not* producing expert results.

Experts *make better choices* than others.

If she's badass, she picks better moves, more often.

↓

Example:

Given a valid position on the board, a chess grandmaster selects a superior move, more reliably, than chess players of a lower rating.

Experts make superior choices

(And they do it more <u>reliably</u> than experienced non-experts.)

Every moment in which the expert is using their expertise ***they're making choices***. Not necessarily *conscious* choices (more on that later), but at any moment, of all the possible things they *could* do, the expert *chooses that which produces superior results*, and the expert does it more consistently than experienced non-experts.

Given a patient with a specific set of symptoms, chooses a more accurate diagnosis, more reliability.

Given a specific software development challenge, chooses a better design and coding approach, more consistently.

Given a specific set of subject and lighting conditions, chooses better composition and exposure options, more consistently.

Given specific, challenging, advanced *slope conditions*, the expert snowboarder chooses a more skillful move more reliably.

Yes, the word "better" is kind of a problem. We'll get to that.

> *But what does "better" even mean?*
> *Who decides THIS "performance" or*
> *"choice" was better than THAT?*

It's up to us to find or create a useful definition of what "better" performance means for our context.

And we must be *specific*. If performance can't be *evaluated* in some way, we can't help someone *build* it. It's not enough to say "experts at [x] do this *better* than non-experts." We must define specific criteria for what it means to *do* or *be* "better."

Given a specific program requirement and constraints, the expert programmer writes **better code,** *more reliably.*

What does this mean? How will we know that THIS code is "better" than THAT code?

Examples of expert "creativity"

Creative work might seem too subjective for defining expertise, but remember, this is about defining *results*.

Given a specific comic theme, an expert comic writer/artist will design more humorous comics, more reliably.

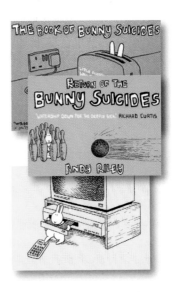

Given the highly specific theme of "bunny suicide," Andy Riley filled more than three volumes with different instances of... bunny suicide. Riley is a reliable bunnicide badass.

Given a specific audience and point in the event, a master DJ will (more reliably) choose and mix music that produces the desired response in the audience.

↑

OK as long as somewhere we've defined what "desired response" means.

Wouldn't this still make the evaluation of "creative results" just a popularity contest?

Remember: *popular* does not necessarily mean *expert*.

In some domains, popularity *is* a key indicator of superior performance, but that's still only *one* of the two criteria for true expertise.

In many creative domains, the extent to which a specific audience appreciates the performance *matters;* it's often at least *correlated* with expertise. But to meet the definition of expertise, an expert must also *sustain* that popularity. They must be able to "be popular" more reliably. In other words, not simply a one-hit-wonder.

We're still left with a question of whether *this* audience is better suited to evaluate performance than *that* audience. Is musical expertise best judged by a panel of the top orchestra players in the world or celebrity talent-show judges? There's no simple answer in domains where "performance" is not measured by objective criteria such as speed or distance.

For helping our users move forward, it's more important that we *have* defined criteria-for-superior-performance, *any* criteria, even if it's not the One True Perfect Objective measure.

Create a definition of badass for your *context*

Template:

Given a *representative task in the domain,* an expert *performs in a superior way* more reliably.

Compelling Context

Specific example (photography)

Given a *specific camera/lens and a specific exposure and composition setting,* a badass **photographer** produces more aesthetically pleasing and evocative photos, more reliably.

For your context:

Given:

describe a representative task

an expert:

describe superior performance for the task

more reliably.

Create a definition of badass for your *tool*

Template:
Given a *representative task in the domain*, an expert *performs in a superior way,* more reliably.

Specific example (camera)
Given a *specific requirement for exposure, focus, and color balance,* a badass **user of this camera** *makes the correct adjustments in the optimal way,* more reliably.

For your tool:

Given:

describe a representative task

an expert:

describe superior performance for the task

more reliably.

Note: you might end up with dozens of these "definitions of badass" depending on how many different tools and contexts apply to your users.

> *We can't just make ANYONE badass. What if they don't have a natural talent/ability/brain/body for our bigger context?*

The myth of "natural talent"

One of the main reasons people don't even *try* to get better at something they'd *like* to do is their belief that *they just don't have what it takes.* Either they *never* had it or they think they've passed an age threshold and now it's too late to learn let alone become badass.

We all have piles of personal evidence to support this: maybe it was something we dreamed of mastering but no matter how hard we worked, we just... didn't. Or we know someone for whom a specific ability emerged with seemingly little effort. "Naturally gifted," we say, "born for this."

As pervasive and intuitive this belief is, there's just one tiny problem: science. Evidence has been mounting for decades that for *most* non-sport domains and for *most* people, "natural talent" is **not** an absolute requirement for reaching high levels of expertise.

A natural talent for focused practice

Other than the sports that depend on specific physical prerequisites, few domains have hard genetic limits for expertise. There *is* a way in which natural ability might contribute to high expertise in non-athletic domains, but it's *not* domain-specific "natural" gifts... it's a natural ability for *focused practice*.

A world-class violin player, for example, *might* have applied her skills for building expertise to chess, skiing, engineering, or nearly *anything* else she chose (assuming she was physically capable). But even without a natural talent for focused practice, we can all learn the meta-skill of *building skill*. People often find that after they've developed a high level of skill in *one* domain, it becomes easier to develop high skill in an entirely *different* domain. They've become badass at becoming badass. And so will our users.

A natural talent for focus and practice means a seemingly "gifted" young musician could likely have chosen any non-music domain instead, and excelled. (Assuming they had the physical prerequisites to do it.)

He picked music... but he could have picked chess, design, programming, rock climbing, etc. etc. etc.

Source: Neuroscientist Richard Restak, *Mozart's Brain and the Fighter Pilot*

<u>THE</u> best vs. <u>ONE OF</u> the best

The big difference (when there is one) between the "naturally talented" and those who aren't typically shows up only at the *edges* of expertise.

Even at the *very* top levels in most non-sport domains, there's little evidence that "natural talent" is a hard requirement. But where it might exist, it's most likely to show up at the beginning of the curve and the very very very top.

And a seemingly "natural talent" is not always an advantage; those who sail effortlessly through the early stages often become deeply discouraged when the faster-than-average pace of their progress suddenly slows or stalls (we'll look more at motivation later).

Again, there *are* some domains—primarily sports—in which natural attributes matter. But even within *those* domains, many *without* those ideal natural attributes still become highly skilled experts.

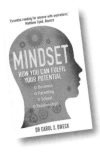

Stanford psychology professor Dr. Carol Dweck has extensive research in motivation that shows, among other things, the damage of labels like "a natural." Her book Mindset should be required reading for anyone who wants to help ANYONE get better at ANYTHING.

But again, most of us will "settle" for being simply really *really* good

Most of us (and our users) would love to simply be *skilled* at something we care about. We don't need to be anywhere near world-class to inspire others to notice we're *better*.

Even just a *little* better can be obvious.

My little indie film won Best Short at Telluride this year.

Your skills took a big jump forward this year!

What about support and encouragement? World-class athletes and musicians often had parents that made sure their kid had the best coaches, training, etc.

Yes, support and encouragement can be crucial.

*That's what **you're** going to do.*

Where you find high expertise, you often *do* find an environment centered around building that expertise.
That usually means access to a good *training* program (school, coach, etc.) and the *time, space, and tools* for practice.

We can't necessarily give our users extra time and space for practice, but as we'll see in the rest of this book, we *can* give them the kind of support and tools that make every learning and practice moment as effective as possible.

> *"My only regret at age 100 is that I should have taken up the violin at age 60.*
>
> *I'd have been playing for **40** years by now."*

If almost anyone can *become expert at almost anything, why do most of us fail to even reach* mediocre *let alone badass? If it's NOT natural talent... what IS it?*

It's time to answer the Big Question.

What did those who *did* become expert do differently from those who wanted to but *didn't?*

The answer to this question not only helps us build badass users, but it's the key to making them better at *every* stage, and in a way that helps them stay motivated to keep going.

Now that we know what expertise *is,* it's time to look at how it's *developed...*

What Experts Do
▼
Science of Badass   ▶**Building Skills**

You can't have expertise without expert *skills*

Imagine you put three posters on the wall, one for each of three skill categories: **Can't** do, Can do **With Effort**, and **Mastered**. Now imagine you make a sticky note for each skill you need to master for that domain.

One of our key roles is helping users move each skill from "**Can't** *do*" to "**Can** *do*." But "*Can do*" comes in two flavors: *with conscious effort* (not reliable) and *mastered* (reliable/automatic).

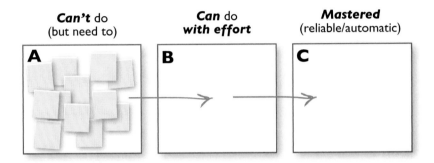

***Can't* do** (but need to)	***Can* do** ***with effort***	***Mastered*** (reliable/automatic)
A	**B**	**C**

Skill: DSLR Photography *Exposure*

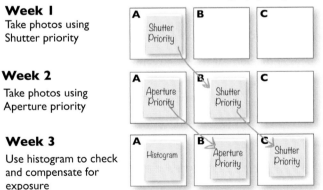

Week 1
Take photos using Shutter priority

A — Shutter Priority | B | C

Week 2
Take photos using Aperture priority

A — Aperture Priority | B — Shutter Priority | C

Week 3
Use histogram to check and compensate for exposure

A — Histogram | B — Aperture Priority | C — Shutter Priority

Is this the best progression for expertise?

Moving from beginner to badass, does *this* sequence make sense for developing expert skills?

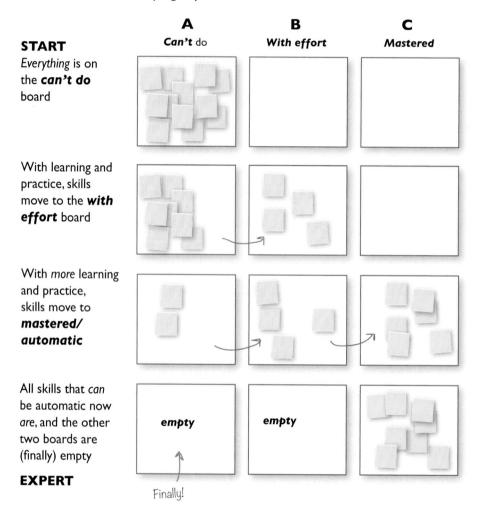

	A **Can't** do	**B** **With effort**	**C** **Mastered**
START *Everything* is on the **can't do** board			
With learning and practice, skills move to the **with effort** board			
With *more* learning and practice, skills move to **mastered/ automatic**			
All skills that *can* be automatic now *are*, and the other two boards are (finally) empty **EXPERT**	*empty* Finally!	*empty*	

(Spoiler Alert: no, this is *not* the path to high expertise.)

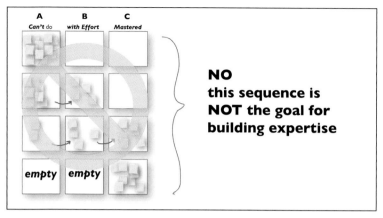

**NO
this sequence is
NOT the goal for
building expertise**

Problem 1:

This sequence shows *only* skills that move from A to B to C. Experts have *some* skills that move from A directly to C.

NOT just this

We also want THIS

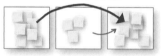

Problem 2:

Experts *never* have an empty A board; they're forever adding new skills (or refinements of existing skills).

NEVER this

We want THIS (always)

Problem 3:

Experts move skills from B to C, but must *also* move skills *backwards* from C to B.

NOT just this

We also want THIS

Wait...what? Why would you ever want to DE-automate a skill you worked hard to master?

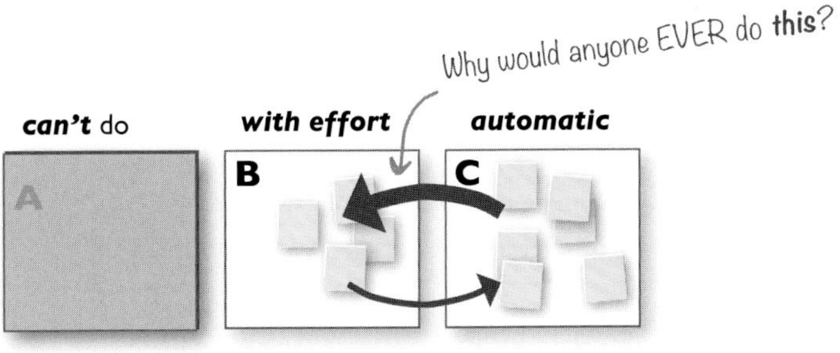
Why would anyone EVER do this?
can't do
with effort
automatic
A
B
C

Unconscious/automated skills are often the cause of "intermediate blues"

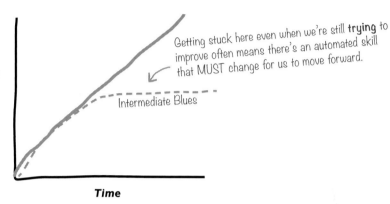

Ability

Getting stuck here even when we're still **trying** to improve often means there's an automated skill that MUST change for us to move forward.

Intermediate Blues

Time

If you're helping people get better at ANY physical activity, sport, etc. you might want to watch the Breakthrough on Skis videos.

Example

Expert ski instructor Lito Tejedas-Flores has been helping people break out of the "intermediate blues" for more than two decades. He found that the secret to breaking through to advanced and expert skiing is about changing just *one* specific *previously-automated skill.* One.

By the time most people are skiing at *intermediate* level, this particular skill is usually unconscious, fully automated, deeply *locked-in.* Fixing it means first bringing it *back* to conscious "inspection" so we can *then* do the hard work of actually *changing* it. (Hint: it's about weight shift)

Another reason to *de*-automate skills:
Use it or lose it is a myth.
Using it is not enough.

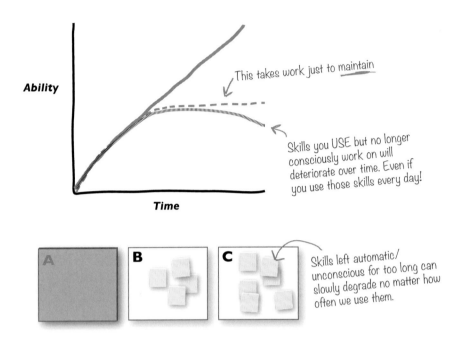

Ability

This takes work just to maintain

Skills you USE but no longer consciously work on will deteriorate over time. Even if you use those skills every day!

Time

Skills left automatic/ unconscious for too long can slowly degrade no matter how often we use them.

If you don't use a skill for a while it becomes rusty. But what about skills you *do* use every day? Many professionals, for example, reach a level of expertise and think, "I can finally quit *practicing* and now just *use* my hard-earned skills."

But something scary happens.

The skills we *use* but don't consciously *practice* can slowly deteriorate, even if we're using them every day. The phrase "use it or lose it" is misleading. *"Using it" is not enough.*

This is how experts build expertise

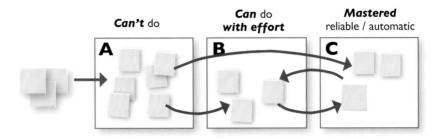

Experts (i.e. those who perform in a superior way, more reliably, in a representative task in the domain) build skills from **Can't do** to **Mastered.**

* Experts never stop adding *new* skills.
* Experts build skills both *consciously* and *unconsciously*.
* Experts *refine* existing skills.

STILL doesn't answer the question... ANYONE can follow this framework, but not everyone becomes badass.

Now we have the right question:

Given this framework, what did experts do differently from experienced *non*-experts who followed the same framework? *(And how can we help our users do this?)*

Those who became experts did two key things differently than experienced non-experts.

The first one won't be a big surprise...

Experts practiced better

What we *think*:

What's actually *true*:

The first common attribute across all domains in which people become badass is this: experts *practice better*.

Those who became experts practiced more effectively than experienced non-experts with the same amount of practice hours.

> *Sorry, but NO.*
> *I practiced **forever** at piano and it didn't make me amazing. It REALLY can't be just "they practiced more."*

It's not *harder* practice
It's not *longer* practice
It's _better_ practice

Practicing harder and longer can potentially make us even *worse* than if we did *less* practicing.

Building deep expertise takes work, but of a **very specific type** that's often the opposite of what most people do when practicing.

*Practice does **not** make perfect.*

In the science of expertise, the form of explicit practice that's known to work effectively is referred to as *Deliberate Practice*.

"Deliberate Practice"
Worst. Name. Ever.

I did thousands of hours of Deliberate Practice to become this good.

Expert

I practiced, deliberately, for *thousands* of hours. Didn't work.

Experienced <u>Non</u>-Expert

Both practiced, deliberately, but in profoundly different ways

"Deliberate Practice"
does *not* mean
"Practice, deliberately"

Mistaking "practicing deliberately" for textbook *Deliberate Practice* has caused much confusion around the significance of practice in expert performance.

Deliberate Practice is usually the best (sometimes *only*) way to *consciously** build skills from *Can't do* to *Mastered*

Deliberate Practice

Moves skills from A to B
(from *can't do* to *with effort*)

Moves skills from B to C
(from *with effort* to *mastered*)

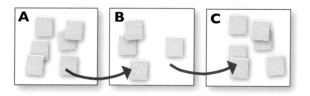

Given an expert and an experienced *non*-expert with the same total hours spent on practice-related activities, the expert has likely spent a greater percentage of those hours in *Deliberate Practice*.

Deliberate Practice fixes the single biggest problem most people have when trying to build expertise...

*Later we'll look at *unconscious* skill building.

The single biggest problem for most people on most expertise curves is having too many things on the **B** board

We try to learn and practice too many things simultaneously instead of nailing one thing at a time.

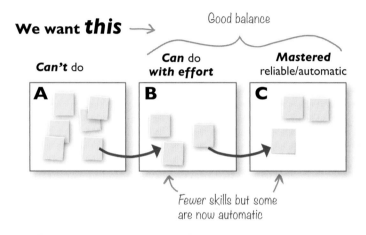

We want *this* → Good balance

Can't do | Can do with effort | Mastered reliable/automatic

A | B | C

Fewer skills but some are now automatic

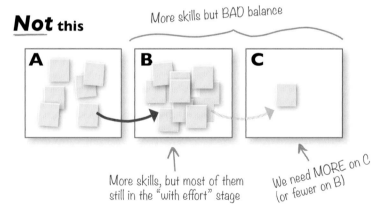

Not this   More skills but BAD balance

A | B | C

More skills, but most of them still in the "with effort" stage

We need MORE on C (or fewer on B)

Deliberate Practice helps prevents what most other forms of practice suffer from:

Pile-up of mediocre skills on *B*

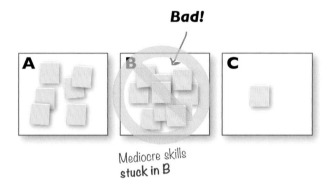

Bad!

Mediocre skills
stuck in B

This pile-up doesn't just *slow* progress, it can *kill* it. Or worse.

Practice activities that are *not* Deliberate Practice can be riskier than just not practicing at all.

The *really* scary thing about practice is...

The more time we spend *practicing mediocre,*
the better we get at... being mediocre.

Practice makes <u>permanent</u>.

Most practice doesn't guarantee better performance.

Most practice *locks-in* whatever is practiced.

We must help our users spend as little time as possible
practicing *being a beginner* at the bigger context (and our tool).

Now we have a big problem: what happens when you're still
in the Suck Zone? How can you practice being *better* than you
actually are? We'll get into that later in the book.

How does Deliberate Practice
help prevent mediocre lock-in?

Deliberate Practice helps prevent lock-in because:

Half-a-Skill beats Half-*Assed* Skills

Mastering one tiny useless-on-its-own sub-skill at a time is nearly always a more effective, efficient way to move explicitly-practiced skills from A all the way to the C board.

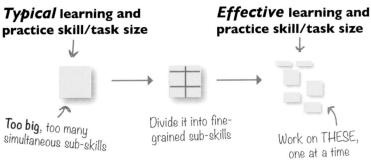

Typical learning and practice skill/task size

↓

Effective learning and practice skill/task size

↓

Too big, too many simultaneous sub-skills

Divide it into fine-grained sub-skills

Work on THESE, one at a time

This

Can't do

Can do with effort

Mastered reliable/automatic

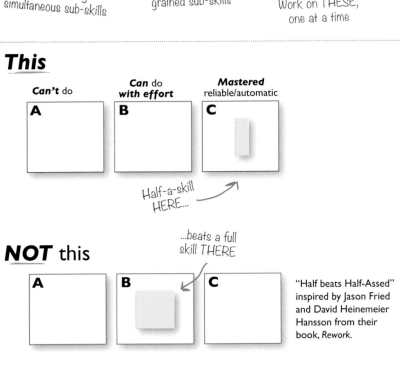

Half-a-skill HERE...

...beats a full skill THERE

NOT this

"Half beats Half-Assed" inspired by Jason Fried and David Heinemeier Hansson from their book, *Rework*.

Exception to Half-a-Skill beats Half-Assed Skills:

For some domains, beginners need a starter set of a *few* half-assed skills

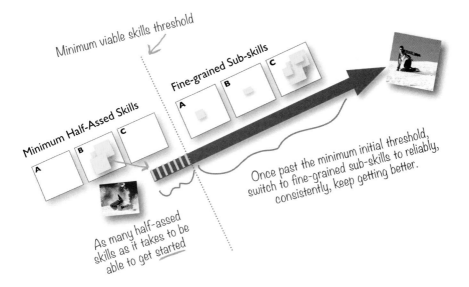

The fine-grained sub-skill approach is usually the most effective way to build skills, but nobody wants to spend the first week riding *only* the bunny slope. For your domain, what's the *minimum viable skill set* for "actually doing the thing"? Your users need as many *fat*-grained, *half-assed* skills as it takes to do at least *something*.

But after they're past the "at least I can do *something*" stage, help them switch to *half*-a-skill beats *half-assed* skills.

Simplified rules for Deliberate Practice
(A *subset* of textbook Deliberate Practice)

Help them practice right

Goal: design practice exercises that will take a fine-grained task from unreliable to 95% reliability, within one to three 45-90-minute sessions

Pick a small sub-skill/task that you *can't* do *reliably* (or at all), and get it to 95% reliability within three sessions. (Getting to 95% in a *single* session is often better).

...and this is different from ordinary practice because...

The difference is in the specific details, and those fine details turn practice that *might* work (or could make things *worse*) into practice that works like a superpower.

NOTE: If you're interested in *other* possibilities for exercises that can work as *Deliberate Practice*, refer to *Cambridge Handbook of Expertise and Expert Performance*.

Deliberate Practice examples

Achieve 95% reliability within one to three 45-90-minute practice sessions

"Shoot the basketball into the hoop while standing 8-12 feet from the hoop at a 45 degree angle."

"Play this section at half speed, without errors."

"Create, compile, and run a program (without errors) that accesses and displays data from this database."

"Create four test blog posts using the Starter Template, with photos inserted at the top and middle of the post."

"Analyze the six cockpit instruments and determine the plane's attitude, within five seconds."

"Shoot *well-exposed* portrait photos using aperture-priority and only natural outdoor lighting in which the subject is back-lit."

Either you can *reliably* play that section at half speed without errors or you can't. Either you can *reliably* determine the plane's attitude within 5 seconds or you can't. Your outdoor natural-light photos are either *reliably* well-exposed or they're not.

If you *can't* get to 95% reliability within three practice sessions...

If you _can't_ get to 95% reliability, _stop trying!_
You need to redesign the sub-skill

The longer we practice an explicit skill that we _can't_ do
reliably, the less likely we are to _ever_ reach mastery. If you
can't get 95% reliability in one to three practice sessions,
change the exercise! Either split the task into a smaller
sub-task, or reduce the performance criteria.

If the task/skill is too _complex_ (too many unmastered skills),
break it into _finer-grained sub-tasks/sub-skills_

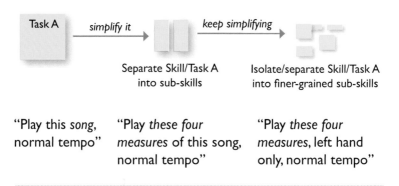

"Play this _song_, normal tempo"	"Play _these four measures_ of this song, normal tempo"	"Play _these four measures_, left hand only, normal tempo"

**If it's _not_ complex but it's too _difficult_, make
the performance criteria _easier_**

"Play these four measures normal tempo"	"Play these four measures _half_-tempo"	"Play these four measures of this [easier] song, as slowly as it takes for 95% accuracy"

Not all practice is Deliberate Practice

Any practice activity for which you do *not* become significantly more reliable in a task or skill within one to three sessions, is *not* Deliberate Practice. Common practice-related activities that *don't* qualify as Deliberate Practice:

* Work on a project. For example, create a small game in a new programming language.

* Work through a step-by-step tutorial.

* Listen to a lecture or presentation.

* Play a complete piece of music, at a speed that you *already* perform *reliably*.

* Play a complete piece of music, at a speed you *won't* be able to perform reliably within three practice sessions.

* A practice exercise for a skill that will take more than one session to become reliable AND there's *too long a gap between sessions*. (Too much time between practice sessions means each subsequent session is virtually a repeat of the first session.)

You CAN'T be saying that tutorials and projects don't work...

Practice that is NOT Deliberate Practice can still be valuable and necessary

Playing/Performing is **not** Deliberate Practice

Play enough games of chess against a stronger opponent and you *will* improve but it could take *forever* compared to an approach that involves both game play *and* Deliberate Practice. *Playing is not practicing,* or at least not the kind of practicing proven to effectively and efficiently build skills.

Step-by-step tutorials are **not** Deliberate Practice

Step-by-step procedural instructions can be the key to figuring out *which* Deliberate Practice exercises to do and *how* to do them. But tutorials are usually *not* Deliberate Practice.

Think of a step-by-step tutorial as *performing by remote control.* You're executing commands given by someone else. Tutorials can give you a feel for the skill you're learning and provide more *context* than your current skills enable. That's extremely valuable, but don't mistake it for the skill-building of Deliberate Practice.

Projects are **not** Deliberate Practice

You *can* learn video editing by making a video. You *can* learn a new programming language by using it to build a game. Projects are a powerful motivator and often a deep, rich learning experience, forcing you to figure things out. But... *still not Deliberate Practice.*

Projects are an excellent learning tool, but they're more about discovery and problem-solving than reliable skill-building.

That 10,000 hours thing

You've probably heard about the "10,000 hour rule" popularized by author Malcolm Gladwell in his bestseller *Outliers*. Two problems:

1. *It's not a rule.*

2. The 10,000 hour *thing-**not**-rule* is *exclusively* about 10,000 hours of *Deliberate Practice*, not 10,000 hours of *any* form of practice-related activity.

What expertise researchers found is that for *some* (not all) non-new domains, in *general*, those who became top experts *often* (not always) had spent *somewhere around* 10,000 hours of textbook Deliberate Practice. Give or take a few *thousand*. Yes, that's a lot of qualifiers.

It does *not* mean anyone who practices for 10,000 hours *will* be an expert.

It does *not* mean you *can't* be an expert with fewer than 10,000 hours of deliberate practice.

It does *not* mean you won't make *further* progress *after* 10,000 hours.

Some *domains* might need far fewer hours to reach the highest levels. Some might need more.

Some *people* take fewer hours, some might need more.

And there *are* other factors; Deliberate Practice is *not* the *complete* answer to expertise. But *many many many* hours of *some* form of Deliberate Practice are *always* required to build deep advanced expertise in a complex domain.

If textbook Deliberate Practice is so much better than other practice, wouldn't EVERYONE already be doing it?

Those who developed deep expertise in a challenging domain did hours and hours and hours of Deliberate Practice

Whether by design (of a good coach, for example), trial and error, or even by accident, those who became expert in domains with a long path to mastery *were* logging Deliberate Practice hours.

Those who tried to get better but *didn't*, despite the same number of hours on practice-related activities, were probably *not* doing the kind of practice that qualifies as Deliberate Practice.

Why not? Why wouldn't every teacher/trainer/coach/mentor/employer—everyone with a stake in our improvement—use textbook Deliberate Practice?

It's complicated...

The *wrong* ways to practice *feel* right

The *wrong* ways to practice make sense.

Most of us have a ton of experience *practicing* practicing.
From music lessons to school sports, all of us have spent time
practicing, and chances are we weren't practicing the *right* things
in the *right* way. In other words, we're all highly experienced at
practicing badly.

Most of us were taught that to practice means *doing more of it
more often.* We're told it's about *putting in the time* and *working
hard.* Most practice does *not* focus on building individual skills
and sub-skills to 95% reliability within one to three practice
sessions.

And when we've been practicing hard but aren't making
progress, we usually blame *ourselves* (or our tools/gear) when
the problem was actually too little *Deliberate Practice* combined
with too much *traditional practice.*

But there's another big reason why
most of us don't practice the right way...

The *right* ways to practice *feel* wrong

Deliberate Practice is *always* just beyond our current ability/
comfort zone.

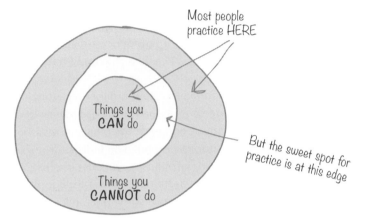

Most people
practice HERE

Things you
CAN do

Things you
CANNOT do

But the sweet spot for
practice is at this edge

Many of us at least subconsciously resist doing what we *can't* do,
even when we *want* to practice and *think* we're practicing.
We keep repeating what we can *already do*, hoping to get
incrementally better by doing more of it.

Or we do the *opposite*, practicing skills *way* past our current
ability. We practice a complex skill for which we haven't yet built
reliability at most of the sub-skills. We practice things we have
no chance of performing well, hoping that if we just keep trying,
one day it'll all somehow come together.

Remember, the more we *practice* being mediocre, the more we
reinforce mediocre skills. Practice makes permanent, so think
carefully about what you're practicing. Think carefully about
what you're encouraging, supporting, helping your *users* do.

Doesn't THAT sound motivating. If building badass users depends on getting our users to do deliberate practice...

There's no escaping at least some Deliberate Practice.

But there's more to this story.

Yes, *some* Deliberate Practice is necessary to build skills. And no, Deliberate Practice is generally *not* fun. (Later in the book we'll look at ways to make it easier and more likely for our users to do the hard work of Deliberate Practice.)

But remember, there are *two* common attributes among experts. *Two* things that people with high expertise did that others *didn't*. Besides the right type of *practice* (Deliberate Practice), master performers did something *else* that didn't *feel* like practice. In fact, they might not have known they were doing anything at all.

This almost-magical second attribute can produce knowledge and skill in powerful, dramatic ways, and in many cases, *better* than any amount of direct instruction or practice.

...and that magical unicorn superpower that makes us better without all that hard practice would be...

That's the next chapter.

What Experts Do
▼
Science of Badass ▶Building Skills ▶**Perceptual Exposure**

1. Experts *practiced* better

2. **Experts were *around* better**

What we *think*:

His parents are pro musicians, he obviously inherited his talent

↓

What's actually *true*:

His parents are pro musicians, so he was surrounded by musicians from an early age

↓

The *second* attribute of those who became experts is this: **they were exposed to high quantity, high quality examples of expertise.**

Where you find deep expertise, you find a person who was *surrounded* by expertise. The more you watch (or listen) to expert examples, the better you can become. The *less* exposure you have to experts or results of expert work, the less likely you are to develop expert skills.

If that were true, I'd be a genius-level musician. Have you even seen my iTunes playlist? And yet...

Simply being exposed to examples of expertise doesn't build expertise unless the exposure meets specific criteria

The kind of "magical" (but not really magical because it's just how brains work) exposure that produces expertise *could* happen by chance.
But we don't want to leave it up to chance.

...still waiting for that magical unicorn superpower...

It all starts with chickens.

To understand perceptual exposure, we'll begin with the most *extreme* example...

Chicken Sexing

Determining the gender of a newborn chick is notoriously tough, but for large commercial chicken farms, the sooner the females are separated from the males, the sooner they can be on the feeding-for-egg-production path. In the early 1900s, the Japanese developed a particular method for chick sexing and a few experts (reliable, accurate chick-sexers) emerged.

Great, we'll have those experts teach others, right? Just one problem: when questioned, the chick-sexing experts didn't know exactly *how* they did it. "I just knew." They were sexing baby chicks with near-perfect accuracy; obviously they *were* using *some* specific criteria to do it. But that precise criteria was not fully or clearly defined, and wanna-be chick-sexers couldn't perceive the subtle unique female chick attributes *even when instructed by experts*. It was as though expert chick-sexers had superhuman vision mere mortals would *never* have.

The key to this story is not that people *did* (and continue to) become experts/masters of chicken sexing...
the key is in how the existing experts "trained" new experts.

Master "chicken sexers" can determine the gender of a newly-hatched chick, instantly, though they may not know how they're doing it.
(baby chicks look identical)

"I just... know."

The real question is... if experts don't know how they do it, how do they train others to do it?

Making *you* a master chick-sexer

I don't know, whatever, OK that one's male, I guess, and I'll say that one's female, but I'm totally **just guessing!**

So how *did* they teach new chick sexers? Imagine *you're* one of the new recruits. You're standing in front of a bin full of baby chicks. You've been given detailed instructions on how to determine male from female based on visual cues. But after your "formal" training, all baby chicks still appear exactly the same to you.

Now you're told to pick one up and just... make a wild guess. "OK, whatever, male" and you put it in the MALE bin, "OK, whatever, I'll guess female" and you put it in the FEMALE bin. *As far as you know, you're doing this randomly.*

After each wild, random, totally made-up guess, the master chick-sexer gives you *feedback.* Yes, no, no, yes. You still have no idea how the expert "knows," but you just keep doing this, over and over.

And then, eventually, something happens. You begin scoring better than random. You get better. Over time, *much* better. *But you don't know why.* For all you know, you're *still* just guessing, but now it's as if some "mysterious" force is guiding your hand toward the correct bin.

Of course there *are* specific, extremely subtle cues that you were using to sort male from female, but you *performed* as an expert *without* consciously recognizing the cues.

Chick sexing is not the *only* example of being expert at something without knowing how you do it

Another example is the friend-or-foe aircraft "spotters" in World War II England. A few civilians were somehow able to instantly distinguish a German plane (on a bombing mission) from a British plane returning home. The British government, *desperate* for spotters, asked expert spotters to train others.

Neuroscientist David Eagleman describes what happened:

"It was a grim attempt. The spotters tried to explain their strategies but failed. No one got it, not even the spotters themselves. Like the chicken sexers, the spotters had little idea how they did what they did—they simply saw the right answer.

With a little ingenuity, the British finally figured out how to successfully train new spotters: by trial-and-error feedback. A novice would hazard a guess and an expert would say yes or no. Eventually the novices became, like their mentors, vessels of the mysterious, ineffable expertise."

"Incognito: the Secret Lives of the Brain"
by Neuroscientist David Eagleman

(recommended)

Your *brain* learns things *you* don't

> I don't know how I do it.
> # I just... *know.*

A master performer appears to have a mystical unexplainable talent, but it's just their brain doing what normal brains do... unconsciously.

It's not magic.
It's *perceptual knowledge.*

As a chick-sexer trainee, you *were* learning. Your *brain* learned from high-quantity exposure to expert performance. Your brain just didn't bother telling *you* what it learned.

After enough exposure with feedback, your brain began detecting patterns and underlying structures, without your conscious awareness. With *more* exposure, your brain fine-tuned its perception and eventually figured out what *really* mattered. Your brain was making finer distinctions and sorting signal from noise even if *you* couldn't explain how.

*It was just your **brain** learning... without bothering **you** with all those pesky details.*

> I got this.

But it's not just for simple ID tasks like chick-sexing or plane-spotting

Experts in all domains develop and use unconscious perceptual knowledge

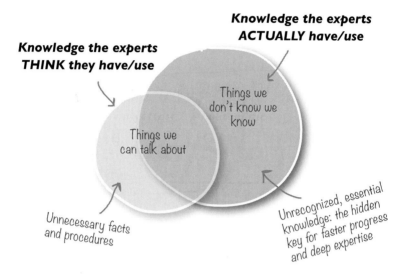

Knowledge the experts THINK they have/use

Knowledge the experts ACTUALLY have/use

Things we don't know we know

Things we can talk about

Unnecessary facts and procedures

Unrecognized, essential knowledge: the hidden key for faster progress and deep expertise

Experts of *all* complex domains share a characteristic with chick-sexers: their brain *knows* much more than it *reveals*. Becoming badass in a complex, challenging domain means acquiring deep pattern recognition beyond conscious awareness.

Perceptual knowledge includes what we think of as expert *intuition*. The ability to instantly know *which* chess move to make. Or that *this* painting is a *forgery*. Or that *this* house fire will *explode*. Or that there's *something* wrong with that code, even though you can't always articulate *how* you know.

> *Still leaves the Big Question: why do some people develop "perceptual knowledge" from exposure, but others don't?*

The reason why some people develop perceptual knowledge from exposure but others don't isn't about the people, it's about the type of exposure.

Remember, simply being exposed to examples of expertise doesn't necessarily build perceptual knowledge unless the exposure meets specific criteria. Though the kind of exposure that produces expertise *could* happen by chance, we *don't want to leave it up to chance.*

What is the criteria for perceptual exposure that leads to perceptual knowledge?

We'll start with another *feels-like-magic-but-isn't* research example, but this one's *far* more complex than chick-sexing and plane-spotting.

Way past chickens:
Perceptual learning in flight training

In 1994 two researchers—Phillip Kellman from UCLA and Mary Kaiser from NASA—presented an astonishing study at the annual Human Factors and Ergonomics Society meeting. The first of two experiments was on aircraft instrument reading.

Non-pilots out-scored seasoned pilots on an instrument reading test after less than two hours of perceptual exposure and less than five minutes of actual instruction.

Fluency with the standard cockpit instruments can be the difference between life and death. Seasoned pilots can glance at the instruments and immediately extract enough information to know the plane's situation. They must also recognize instrument *failure*, when two or more instruments give conflicting information. *Both* speed and accuracy matter. But for novice pilots, this takes effort, and a slower, tedious look at *each* separate instrument, analyzing each one at a time.

Kellman and Kaiser designed a perceptual learning experiment around "information pick-up" from flight instruments. Participants viewed a cockpit instrument display, then chose one of seven responses:

Straight and level

Straight climb

Straight descent

Level turn

Climbing turn

Descending turn

Instrument conflict (malfunction)

The results were astonishing

Within two hours, non-pilots were faster at accurately interpreting the cockpit instruments than seasoned pilots with an average of more than 1,000 hours flight experience.

Think about that.

These weren't *novice* pilots, these were *non*-pilots with *no* prior knowledge or experience with flight, aeronautics, and instruments. Yet within just *two hours* they were performing a crucial skill *better* than experienced pilots.

Of course this didn't mean they could fly a plane, but if they were to start flight training, they'd have a dramatic head start on a crucial skill. With instrument perception at such a high level, they could focus their effort learning and practicing *other* things.

The perceptual training these non-pilots experienced compressed what typically takes more than a thousand *hours*, into just 120 *minutes!*

The biggest surprise of all? The non-pilots received **less than five minutes of actual instruction**. Just a quick orientation on the instruments. The actual "training" was another variation of chick-sexing: repeated exposure with feedback. The perceptual training consisted of two sessions, each lasting under an hour. Each of the two sessions included 216 trials, divided into 9 blocks of 24 trials per block. Even more remarkable, the feedback was only given at the *end* of each 24-trial block (when they were told both the speed and accuracy of their attempts). The participants made these dramatic improvements with a total of 432 trials.

Their *other* experiment was equally astonishing

Non-pilots out-scored seasoned pilots on a navigation test after just three hours of perceptual exposure, and with no navigation instruction beyond an explanation of the symbols on an aeronautical chart.

In the navigation experiment, subjects were shown a 20-second video of a wide-angle view from the front of a Cessna 182, at an altitude of 2000 feet. After watching the video, they were asked to choose the location of the plane from three possible grid locations on an aeronautical chart. Both speed and accuracy were measured, and they were given feedback after each attempt.

These *non*-pilots received *no* direct instruction on navigation, just a short introduction to the basic symbols used in the aeronautical charts.

The perceptual "training" was simply this: 180 total trials of "watch the cockpit video and choose the grid location on the aeronautical chart." As with the cockpit instrument test, the trials were broken into blocks of 9, and the entire set took two 90-minute sessions. That's it. 180 minutes, 180 "tests" of "watch the video, choose the location, get feedback."

At the end of the three hours, the *non*-pilots were *more* accurate, and slightly *faster* than pilots with hundreds of hours flight experience.

What made the pilot map and instrument perceptual learning exercises work?

Both of these exercises were carefully designed to help the brain "discover" the deeper underlying patterns and structure.

When given a *large* set of *diverse* examples, your brain begins to detect *that which does not vary.* There was something–some *invariant* attribute–among chicks of one sex that the chick-sexer's *brain* eventually perceived, even if the chick-sexer had no conscious awareness. The same was true for the plane-spotters; their brains perceived a deep pattern without letting the plane-spotter know, explicitly, what the pattern was.

But this brain superpower for pattern-matching comes with a few downsides including "discovering" patterns that aren't actually there. For the brain to find deep underlying *accurate* patterns, the example set must be large!

What "large" is depends on many factors, but always err on the side of *more examples.* Many, many, *many* more. Without a high quantity of diverse examples, the brain can't separate signal from noise... it doesn't have enough information to be certain that **this** and **ONLY this** is the *invariant* attribute/pattern.

To design a good perceptual exposure activity that can help the brain find a deep accurate pattern, use **a high *quantity* of high *quality* examples that *seem* different on the surface, but actually *aren't.***

Example: *look at these photos*

Pretend you've never learned a thing about photography or design, but want to take better photos. Look at the following photos. Just *look*. Don't try to judge, evaluate, or analyze them. *You won't be asked to explain anything about them.* Just *look* at them. *All of them.*

(But imagine there are *400+* photos, not just these *six*)

They *look* different, but *aren't*.

Or rather, they have at least one key attribute that is the same across all of the photos

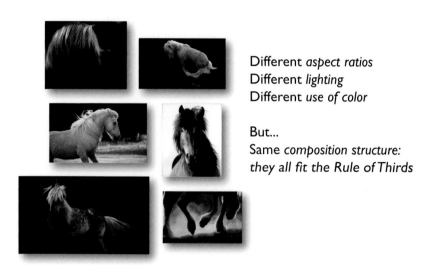

Different *aspect ratios*
Different *lighting*
Different *use of color*

But...
Same *composition structure:*
they all fit the Rule of Thirds

Imagine you want to help someone improve their photographic composition, and the first skill you choose is *Rule of Thirds*. The typical approach to teaching it is to just *explain* it. It takes only a moment to describe, and it's simple to understand and apply. You show some photos with a Rule of Thirds overlay and... *that's it.* Done.

Or is it?

They've learned the *mechanics* of a composition rule, but...

"Rule of Thirds"

Good Perceptual Exposure exercises don't explain. They create a context that lets the learner's brain "discover" the pattern

With photographic composition, it's not really the *mechanics* we're after—it's the *aesthetics*. You've probably seen photos from people who were *taught* the Rule of Thirds, but who never developed a "feel" for composition.

But if we create an experience that helps their brain "discover" composition patterns from looking at high quality, varied examples, we move from just *mechanics* to something *more*... something deeper, richer, and unexplainable.

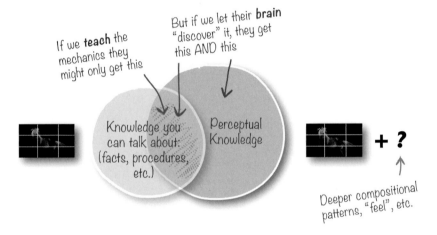

If we **teach** the mechanics they might only get this

But if we let their **brain** "discover" it, they get this AND this

Knowledge you can talk about: (facts, procedures, etc.)

Perceptual Knowledge

+ ?

Deeper compositional patterns, "feel", etc.

For areas where perceptual learning can be used, "they were *taught* it" is not as powerful as "they *discovered* it."

What if they never DO "get it"?
What if they never have that a-ha moment?
What if they stare at 1,000 photos and still
don't "discover" the Rule of Thirds?

Pattern discovery is often subconscious

Even if *they* can't describe what they "learned" (or they don't think they've learned anything at all), we might be able to test whether their *brain* learned.

For example, we could compare photos they took before and after the exercise. If their *after* photos demonstrate *better* composition, the exercise still worked. Their *brain* learned even if it didn't bother telling *them* what it discovered.

If the exercise *did* fail (they did *not* learn from the perceptual exposure), the most likely causes are:

- *not enough examples*
- *not enough diversity in the examples*
- *too long a gap between exposure and feedback*
- *attribute/pattern was **too** subtle*

Making a minimum viable Perceptual Exposure Experience for your users

You don't need to be the expert. *You* don't necessarily need to know the deep underlying patterns for your bigger context/ domain. *You* don't need to know why X is an example of expertise but the similar-looking Y is considered mediocre.

You just need to expose your users to a high quantity of high quality examples, within a compressed time.

Remember, the main goal is to *get* better by being *exposed* to better. In the photography example, we can use photos even if *we* don't know the underlying invariant ourselves. The most effective thing we can do for our users is increase the quantity of examples that demonstrate high expertise.

How can you show these examples? It depends on the domain. For photography, you don't need to show the expert photographer actually *taking* photos, you can simply show the *resulting photos.* You don't need to show a programmer writing code, you can simply show lots and lots and lots of "good" code (again, for whatever definition of "good" you're using).

But for some domains you might need to show the expert actually performing, demonstrating, making choices. Imagine you make an app to help people design presentations, and the bigger context you've chosen is *public speaking*. You could show examples of good PowerPoint slides, but it might be more powerful to compile a large collection of short video clips of high-quality public speaking.

And again, one *big* example does not make an effective perceptual exposure activity. Far better to have 40 different 2-minute clips of *different* expert presenters than a single 80-minute video of *one* excellent presentation.

WARNING! Don't expose them to examples of *bad*

Think of the brain as an automated recording and mimicking device that learns from exposure, *but*—and this is the scary part—it typically learns *best* what it records the *most.*

Even when *we* know (consciously) that we're seeing examples of bad or beginner quality, our *brain* might not get the memo. Worse, our brain is not just failing to distinguish bad from good, it's actively *learning* and *trying to imitate* those bad examples.

It says *that's* an example of *good.*
And hmmm, OK, it says *this* one is an example of *bad,* and then...

I'm NOT interested in *your judgements,* I'm just trying to pick-up the pattern.

The brain can excel at information pick-up
while "ignoring" the good vs. bad labels.

When you *do* show examples of wrong/bad, make them *feel* wrong/bad

Attach something to the bad example to make it evoke a visceral *"something's wrong"* feeling.

If it's a photograph or video, apply a harsh ugly filter or graphic overlay.

If it's text, put it over a universal NO sign or a skull and crossbones.

Simply using the *words* "bad" or "wrong" or "don't" might not be enough warning to ensure the *brain* gets the message.

Lito Tejedas-Flores uses the "make bad examples feel bad and good examples feel good" in his videos. Examples of *good* skiing appear over and over with simple, elegant, beautiful filming and background music. The few examples of *wrong* have a harsh video filter, and play *without* the beautiful background and music. Even without hearing the explanations in the video, just the look and feel of the images implicitly evokes what to do and what to avoid.

What if the learner MUST be able to identify bad examples? Why can't the perceptual excercise be like chick sexing except instead of identifying male vs. female they identify good vs. bad?

The best way to learn to spot "bad" is by learning the underlying patterns of "good"

"play I like to music." Is something wrong with that sentence? What, exactly, is wrong? If English is your native language, you don't need to know which grammar rules were broken to know, instantly, that it's *not* right. You did *not* need to explicitly learn to spot incorrect sentence construction for your brain to recognize "This is definitely *not* right!"

This doesn't mean we *can't* teach using examples of bad, but the best, safest place for that approach is long *after* the learner develops strong perceptual knowledge for what's *good*. Once they're reliable at perceiving *good*, they'll *automatically* recognize *bad* as "that which doesn't fit the pattern" (even if they can't explain why).

Teach people to recognize bad/wrong/errors by developing and strengthening their recognition of good/right/correct.

That photo was altered! I don't know how, exactly, but something's not right...

And now we have our two key attributes

Those who become experts differ from non-experts with the same amount of experience in two main ways:

1. Experts practice better
   (with activities that meet the criteria for Deliberate Practice)

2. Experts develop deep perceptual knowledge and skills through high-quantity, high-quality exposure with feedback

Review Summary:
What Experts Do

The difference between *experts* and experienced, competent, *non*-experts

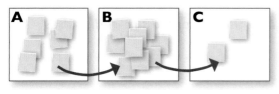

Linear, one-way progression from A to B to C.

Poor balance between B and C, with too many skills/tasks on the B board.

Experts

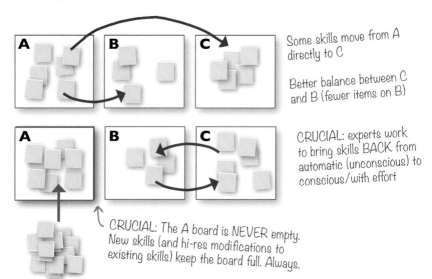

Some skills move from A directly to C

Better balance between C and B (fewer items on B)

CRUCIAL: experts work to bring skills BACK from automatic (unconscious) to conscious/with effort

CRUCIAL: The A board is NEVER empty. New skills (and hi-res modifications to existing skills) keep the board full. Always.

Deliberate Practice examples

 Help users practice right

Achieve 95% reliability within one to three 45-90 minute practice sessions

Break a skill/task into finer-grained sub-skills/tasks

If you can't get to 95% reliability within three 45-90 minute sessions, try breaking the task/skill into smaller sub-tasks/sub-skills until you get to something you *can* master within that time.

Examples

Create a new video project with both an L and J cut.

Modify an existing project with a J cut.

Modify an existing project with two or more cuts.

Create, compile, and run programs that calculate and print values based on command-line args.

Modify the example code to use command-line args. Compile and run.

Compile and run sample programs using command-line args.

Benefits of Perceptual Exposure

A to C
(can't do straight to mastered)

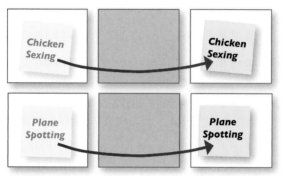

Perceptual exposure can move *some* skills from A to C **without conscious awareness of what was learned or how it was learned.**

"*I just know.*"

A to B *and* A to C

Perceptual exposure can move *some* parts of a complex skill from A to B while simultaneously moving *other* parts of the skill straight from A to C. That **frees up cognitive resources** more quickly.

(We'll look more at cognitive resources later.)

A to B to C *faster* and *better*

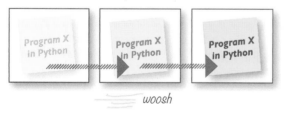

Perceptual exposure can move *all* skills from A to B to C more **quickly**. More importantly, the mastered skills are **higher quality** than they would be without perceptual exposure.

Perceptual Exposure builds capabilities beyond what you think you're learning

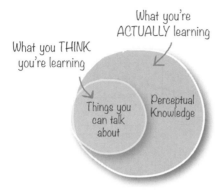

What you're ACTUALLY learning

What you THINK you're learning

Things you can talk about

Perceptual Knowledge

This *is not the whole story of perceptual exposure*

Photograph Sunsets

sub-skill

sub-skill

The sub-skill you ARE consciously aware of, but you don't know HOW you "suddenly just got it."

It's actually more like **this** →

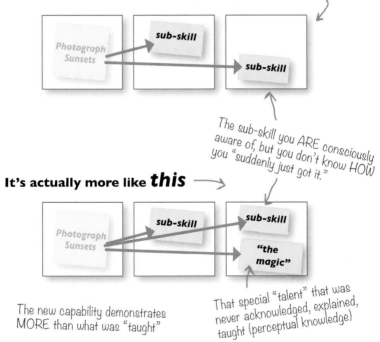

Photograph Sunsets

sub-skill

sub-skill

"the magic"

The new capability demonstrates MORE than what was "taught"

That special "talent" that was never acknowledged, explained, taught (perceptual knowledge)

This is all nice and wonderful, oh look, we're moving skills across the boards, etcetera. But NOTHING matters if our users don't actually DO these things.

You're right. Our formula must include helping our users make steady progress, and that means helping them stay motivated to *want* to.

Don't panic.

This is easier than it sounds.

You can start to make a big
difference for your users
immediately with nothing more
than a simple page or two on
your website.

Help Them Move Forward
▼
Remove Blocks

How do we help users keep moving forward?

Obvious. We entice them with a compelling, engaging, seductive promise/goal to keep pulling them forward.

Enticing goal/promise

Are you sure?
Is the path to creating badass users all about *pulling them forward?*

Maintaining a positive, motivating goal for our users is important, but there's something *more* important. Our users are *already* motivated by the compelling goal. They *want* to get better.

So, if the answer to keeping our users moving forward is *not* about *pulling* them, what is it?

The key question is not, "*What pulls them forward?*"
It's **"What makes them stop?"**

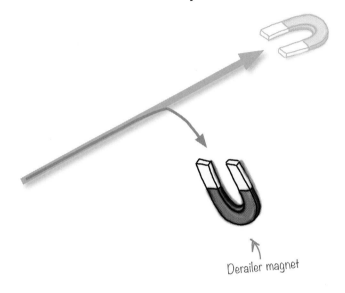

Derailer magnet

They're at least a *little* motivated.

They take steps along the path.

But then they stop. Something derails them.

What do we do about *that*?

Common response:

"Let's make the forward-pulling magnet even bigger and stronger!"

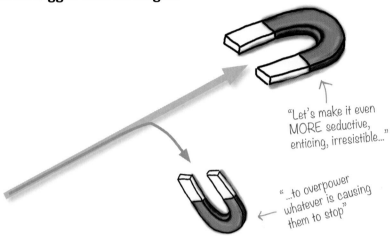

"Let's make it even MORE seductive, enticing, irresistible..."

"...to overpower whatever is causing them to stop"

A typical response to users dropping out is "let's double-down on the forward-pulling magnet." Deeper discounts. Promoting more enticing benefits. Turning the seduction dial to 11.

Besides potential ethical issues with this approach, it's not solving the real problem. It assumes that our user once *had* motivation to do this, but that they somehow *lost* that motivation.

What if it's not a motivation problem?

Remember, our user took the first step. *They wanted the benefits of being better.* Chances are, we do not have a problem for which *more external motivation* is the answer.

Working on what *stops* people matters more than working on what *entices* them

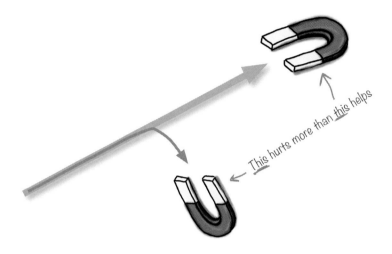

What pulled them off the forward path?

What's *more* compelling than the forward-pulling magnet?

What's *more* powerful than whatever motivated them to start on this path?

Once they've started on the path, the "secret" to helping them move forward is to **focus on reducing what slows or stops them.**

A gap between what they wanted and what's actually happening

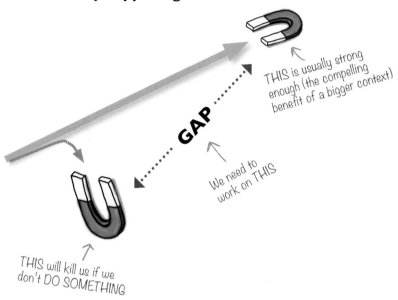

THIS is usually strong enough (the compelling benefit of a bigger context)

We need to work on THIS

THIS will kill us if we don't DO SOMETHING

GAP

They took the first steps. They *are* motivated. They'd *like* (maybe *love*) to be better at the bigger context.

But something derails them. And that something lives in the gap between the already-motivating compelling context and where they are *now*. What causes the gap? What can we do about it? What if we can't close the gap?

There are two big derailer gaps...

The Challenge   What Experts Do   **Help Them Move Forward**
▼
Remove Blocks

The Gap of Suck

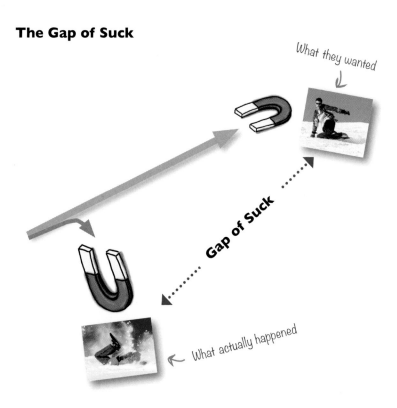

What they wanted

Gap of Suck

What actually happened

If we make/sell snowboards, we don't want to sell just this *one* snowboard, we want to create a snow*boarder*.

The Suck Zone is guaranteed pain for *everyone* learning to snowboard. But those who drop out early didn't suddenly *lose* their motivation to *be a good snowboarder*. They don't need *more convincing* about the features and benefits of snowboarding. They don't need a bigger, sexier forward-pulling magnet.

We must help our users through the large, painful gap between the motivating goal and their early experiences in the Suck Zone.

The Gap of Disconnect

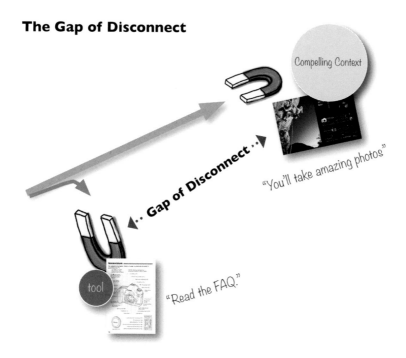

Before they buy/join we're all about the **Context**.
This is where motivation *lives*.

After they buy/join we're all about the **Tool**.
This is where motivation *dies*.

They didn't lose *motivation* for the context. They lost the *connection* between the compelling context and the tool. And they no longer trust that we'll help them with anything but the tool.

Death by a thousand derailers

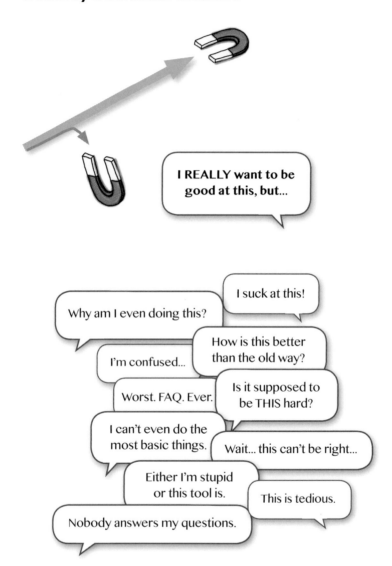

What happens when you can't shrink the gap?

> *OK, fine. We get it. Mind the gaps, etcetera. But what happens if we can't fix the gap?*

> *Snowboarding IS hard the first day. What do we do when we can't change that?*

You're right.

But even if we can't *close* the gap, it doesn't mean we can't help our users while they're in it.

The answer is not to *eliminate* the gap, but to make the gap *no big deal*. The answer is to help users move forward *despite* the gap.

The first step is understanding what the derailers have in common...

What do these derailers have in common?

Assume our user *wants* to get better at the bigger context, and it's possible for them, but they're being pulled off the path by one or more of these:

What's the *common attribute* across all the different thoughts, feelings, and experiences that could derail our users? If we can find a common *attribute*, maybe we can find a common *solution*.

Think about it

If a user could express these thoughts, feelings, concerns, *as they happen,* and you were with them, you could do something to help them.

The common attribute: **we're not there with them when they're thinking and feeling this, and if we were, we'd be able to do something about it.**

← The problem is NOT that they're making this face, it's that we're not there to notice and do something about it.

To think of it another way, what **can't** they tell us because we're *not* right there with them?

They **can't**....

They can't do *this:*

They can't **make that face.**

They can't **ask that question.**

Of course technically they *can*, but we're not there to notice. And if we're not there to notice (and take action), we've removed their ability to communicate their frustrations and questions to someone who can do something about it.

> But we CAN'T be there to notice. And we can't help them with a thought/feeling that we don't even know they're having.

Are you sure?

Are you certain that if you're not there you can't really *know* what they're experiencing?

Are you certain that if you're not there you can't *help* them with what they're experiencing?

For a few moments, pretend you *could* be there to notice the moment they have a question, look confused, frustrated, etc. and then imagine what you could do to help.

The answer begins with figuring out what *would* help them if you *were* there.

Why *does* anyone snowboard the *second* day?

We know *something* pulled them to the slopes that *first* time. They *are* motivated. But that first day ends in pain, frustration, failure, and embarrassment.

And yet... some people *do* go back. They go back *despite* the massive, humiliating, excruciating Gap of Suck.

Snowboarding *is* really hard the first day.
It just *is*.

For anything worth becoming badass at,
there will be pain.

Whether it's the first day of snowboarding,
or first week of programming, our users
will struggle.

The secret for keeping them going when
things get tough is this: ***acknowledge it.***

Some things are just hard.

Why he *did* snowboard the second day

Snowboarder's trusted friend

Dude. ***Everyone*** sucks the first day. ***Everyone.*** But the second or third day, ***everyone suddenly gets so much better.*** Google it. It's totally a thing.

Someone convinced him that snowboarding only *appears* to be an endless bowl of pain, humiliation, and failure. Someone convinced him *he's exactly where he should be and it gets better.*

If you make snowboards, everything associated with your beginner gear should be infused with the First Day Sucks, Second Day Gets Better message. Everything. User manual, follow-up email, in-store posters, Facebook posts, initial marketing brochure—*everything*.

Everything the new snowboarder sees should emphasize:

"Your first day will be frustrating and painful. But here's what's gonna happen..."

Typically, we do the opposite. The more painful we know it will be for them, the more we emphasize the "OMG awesomeness of snowboarding!" We're afraid to even hint at the painful first-day experience.

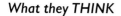

> *How does it make it better to acknowledge its hard? They KNOW it's hard.*

What they THINK

What's ACTUALLY true

> *I must be an idiot.*

> *This part is hard. For everyone.*

The main reason people stop when they're struggling is *not* because they're *struggling*.

It's because they don't know that struggling is *appropriate*.

It's because they don't know that they're exactly where they *should* be.

It's because they don't know that *everybody* struggles at this point.

Just tell them

If they don't know it's normal to struggle at this point, they have no reason to believe it will get better.

If they don't know it's normal to struggle at this point, they have no reason to keep going despite the struggle.

If they don't know it's normal to struggle at this point, they have no reason to feel the struggle is worth it.

Struggling, but willing to try again

OK, fine. I'll try again. Not sure I buy your whole "it'll all come together soon you'll see trust me" thing, but I'll give it a little more time.

← He's really really really hoping you're NOT lying about it (or overestimating his potential) because he'd still love to be good at this. He'd still love for it to work and be worth it.

They stop *not* because of the struggle. They stop because they don't realize the struggle is **typical** and **temporary**.

But what if it's mostly OUR fault they're struggling THIS much? What if part or all of the struggle IS because of something in our product or crappy manual or whatever...

Just Tell Them.

It matters less *why* they're struggling than *that* they're struggling. Obviously you'll do what you can to fix the unnecessary pain caused by problems with your product or support. But until then, *Just Tell Them*.

They don't need you to be *perfect*.

They need you to be *honest*.

If you tell them "here's the problem you're going to struggle with and seriously, it's not you, it's us, but here's what's gonna happen..." their confidence and trust in both you and themselves goes up. Way up.

What's much, much *worse* than a bad user manual?

Making the user think the manual works just fine for everyone else.

> No, really, it's NOT me. It's YOU.
> YOU are what's wrong.
> Nobody *else* has a problem with me.

Don't make users feel this way

The big problem is not that the manual is hard (or bad). The problem is that we act as though it's not.

You can fix that problem immediately *without* fixing the manual.

Just Tell Them.
Try it. It's like a superpower. Not for you, for *them*. As you'll see later in the book, restoring confidence helps free up more of their cognitive resources to actually *think* and *do* more.

Derailer solution:
Anticipate and **Compensate**

Anticipate the most likely faces they might make and questions they might ask if you *were* next to them when they use your product and/or work at the bigger context.

Compensate for their inability to show and tell you what they're experiencing, and more importantly for *your* inability to notice and respond.

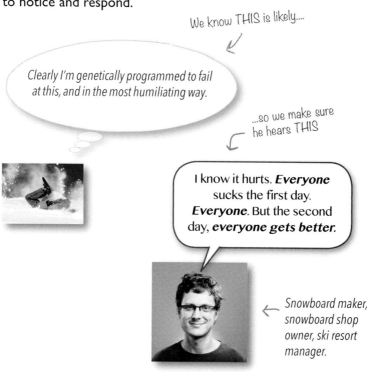

We know THIS is likely....

Clearly I'm genetically programmed to fail at this, and in the most humiliating way.

...so we make sure he hears THIS

I know it hurts. *Everyone* sucks the first day. *Everyone*. But the second day, *everyone gets better.*

Snowboard maker, snowboard shop owner, ski resort manager.

We don't NEED to be with a first-time snowboarder to KNOW they're suffering. It's easy to anticipate THAT. But what if we make software?

It's *obvious* that first-day snowboarders will struggle, but how can we ever know what "faces" and "questions" are happening in most *other* user experiences? How can we *compensate* for that which we can't possibly *anticipate*?

Snowboarding

We know THIS is likely....

Software

...but how could we anticipate THESE?

We don't need to know it's happening.

We just need to *act* as though it is.

Everything? We're to act as though they are making all those faces? Act as though they are asking all those questions? Act as though they are bored, frustrated, skeptical, confused, angry, nervous, tired, and...?

Err on the side of compensating.

It's far better to assume it *is* happening even when it's *not*, than to *not* acknowledge it when it *is*.

One of the *best* places to find what they might be thinking, feeling, experiencing is usually...

Online Discussion Forums (as many as possible)

The best places to uncover what you must compensate for are usually online discussion forums.

(You typically find more open, frank discussions on independent user group sites rather than a company's own tech support site).

Within 15 minutes you'll usually have a clue where the pain and opportunities are, just by scanning for the topics with the highest view and reply counts.

You'll probably find many different forums around the compelling context (vs. your specific tool). The key is to look at as many different forums as you can find, to have the best chance of surfacing the big issues.

(Don't rely on just one site or group)

Depending on your tool, you might also find tool-specific discussions, though they are often sub-topics on a bigger context forum. For example, many photography forums have sub-topics for each of the most popular cameras. If not, you'll have to search in domain (context) forums to see if/where/how people are discussing your specific tool.

What jumps out?

Imagine the bigger context for your product is business modeling/forecasting. Part of that involves spreadsheets, probably Excel. Now imagine you visit the Excel User Group online forum and scan the front page. What do you see?

(Note: be especially careful about *old* discussions that still *appear* "hot" because of a recent post.)

Look for unusually high numbers

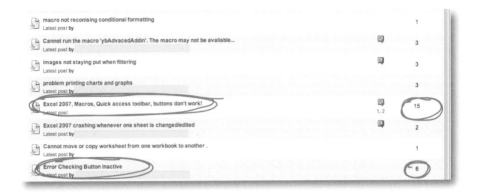

In less than 10 seconds, we learn:

"The Quick access toolbar, buttons don't work" is a hot topic with more than twice the replies of anything else on the page.

(Note: everything in these forum screenshots is most likely out of date by the time you're reading this. Assume everything written more than one week ago might be out of date, already fixed, or no longer relevant.)

"Error Checking Button inactive" is the second-hottest topic.

All the questions are about problems using the software.

The questions that have *no* replies are probably not problems for most users.

What can we learn with one glance?

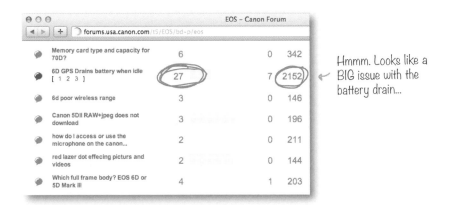

Hmmm. Looks like a BIG issue with the battery drain...

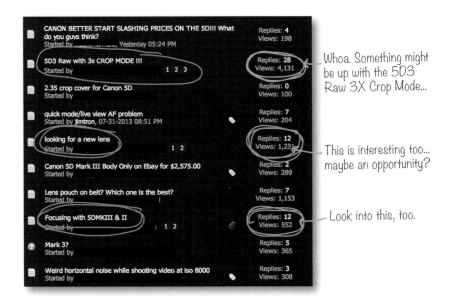

Whoa. Something might be up with the 5D3 Raw 3X Crop Mode...

This is interesting too... maybe an opportunity?

Look into this, too.

And now that we've learned what could be a problem...

Compensate

Don't hide it or deny it. Either fix something that makes that problem go away completely or *Just Tell Them*.

Tell them in as many ways and places as you can:

• *User manual*

• *Marketing*

• *Support web site*

• *Community / User Groups*

• *Product/context blogs*

• *YouTube videos*

• *In-store posters* ("everyone sucks the first day snowboarding")

• *Product user interface*

• *Testimonials* (most testimonials are the opposite of what users need to hear)

• *Case studies and examples with lessons learned*

• *New User training, seminars, etc.*

Just tell them.

"We're being honest with you—this matters. It's not going to be easy."

"What our marketing promised you'd be able to do? We'll help you do that. It's going to be harder than our website makes it sound."

"Everyone who stuck with it has gone through what you're going through. It's typical and temporary."

"It's not you. It's us. But you won't have to do this alone."

Be brave.

Help Them Move Forward
▼
Remove Blocks   ▶**Progress + Payoffs**

We looked at what pulls them *off* (derailers) but what pulls them <u>forward</u>?

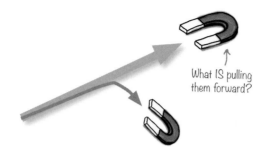

What IS pulling them forward?

We had this discussion, remember? We're supposed to assume they're already motivated by the bigger context, and focus on what stops progress rather than trying to add motivation.

Right.

The answer is *not* "more seductive marketing or incentives."

But though the promised *goal*—badass skills/results—is still *motivating*, sometimes it feels like it'll take *forever* to get there.

What happens between Day One and Total Badass?

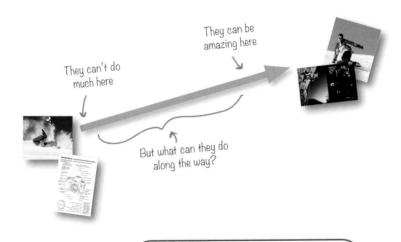

I know it would be phenomenal and I would **love** to get there, but it takes *years* and I heard you can't do anything useful or interesting until you're **really** good.

The benefits of badass can't come only at the *end*

We paint a compelling picture of how amazing it will be when they're experts with all that high resolution and skill, but what can they do *tomorrow*?

It doesn't matter if our users are getting better unless they *know* they're getting better and *benefit* from getting better.

Where **am** I now?
What can I **do** now?

To help users stay motivated, give them:

- A description of the path with guidelines to help them know where they are at each step.

- Ideas and tools to help them *use* their current skills early and often.

Performance Path Map: a key to motivation and progress

Whether it was a trusted coach who said, "Do exactly what I say, and you *will* get better." or a credible progress system like martial arts, those who became badass had something (or someone) to follow.

An ideal Performance Path Map:

- Clear steps of progression from beginner to badass.

- A way to assess where you are relative to the full map. "You are **here**."

- A credible reason to believe it works, and confidence that it can work *without* "natural talent" or spectacular luck.

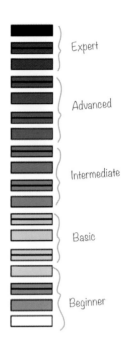

Expert

Advanced

Intermediate

Basic

Beginner

The martial arts belt system is a clear, credible path map that defines each step along the way, includes a way to assess progress, and provides increasing benefits and capabilities at each step/level/belt.

A Performance Path Map is about what you *do*, not what you *learn*

The International Kiteboarding Organization (IKO) offers training courses with level progressions from entry/recreational to professional

Discovery - Kiteboarder Level 1 on land (2-4 hours)

Level 1A - Site Selection

- Know safe wind directions and conditions for kiting
- Know hazards on a spot
- Set up a trainer kite
- Know the use of safety systems
- Carry and handle the kite properly

Level 1B - Basic Piloting

- Have basic flying skills with trainer kite
- Launch and land the trainer kite with an assistant
- Twist and untwist the lines while flying the kite
- Walk and change directions while flying the kite
- Know the wind window

Level 1C - Control Systems

- Set-up a 4/5 line kite with a full de-power system
- Pre-flight check of equipment and settings
- In flight check of equipment and settings
- Pull quick release and activate leash
- Understand and use the international communication signals
- Launch and land the kite to an assistant and as an assistant (4/5-line de-power kite)

Level 1D - Power Control

- Control the kite hooked into the harness
- Understand the de-power system and can use the safety systems
- Advanced flying skills with the de-power kite
- Show full control of de-power systems in flight

Level 1E - Self Landing

- Self land
- Recover the bar and kite

THIS is how a Performance Path Map should look: <u>skills</u>, not just knowledge

The problem with most learning and mastery paths is they define what you should *learn*, not what you will *do*.

A learning/mastery path that tells you what course to take next, book to read, or topic to study is still better than *nothing*, but it's far more effective if we map topics-learned directly to mastered-skills.

Remember that we also need a "GPS" for the map. There *must* be a clear way for users to figure out what they can now do and where they now are on the map.

Just *knowing* a Performance Path *exists* is a strong motivator

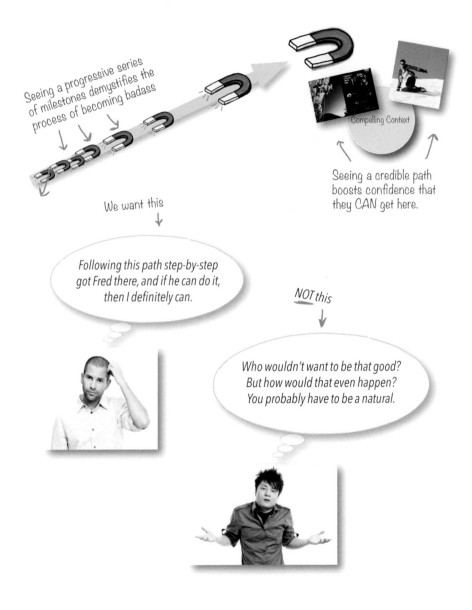

Seeing a progressive series of milestones demystifies the process of becoming badass

Compelling Context

Seeing a credible path boosts confidence that they CAN get here.

We want this

Following this path step-by-step got Fred there, and if he can do it, then I definitely can.

NOT this

Who wouldn't want to be that good? But how would that even happen? You probably have to be a natural.

Find or make a Performance Path Map for your context domain

To find an existing path:

- Professional organizations and industry-standards groups
- College degree program curriculums
- Active user groups and discussion forums
- Table of Contents from "The Definitive Guide" (whatever people refer to as "the *bible* of this")

To create a path:

Make a list of key skills ordered from beginner to expert, then slice them into groups to make ranks/levels. For motivation, the earlier, lower levels should be achievable in far less time and effort than the later, advanced levels. One possibility is to have each new level take roughly double the time and effort of the previous level.

Each rank above black belt in the ancient game of Go is thought to take twice the knowledge/skill/effort of the previous level

Experts fight over which path is best/right

Everybody gets it wrong. If you want to learn this right, you HAVE to get good at THIS first. There's no other way.

Expert A

Dude. That's ridiculous. Nobody will ever get anywhere if they do THAT first. They need THIS...

Expert B

Guys, guys, you're both being silly. What REALLY matters is that they do THESE things first. Everyone knows this.

Expert C

How do you choose? How can beginners trust a "credible path" when even the experts cannot agree on *which* knowledge and skills *matter* let alone the *order* in which knowledge and skills should be learned?

It's OK.

Experts disagree on the right path because they probably don't actually know (but *believe* they *do*)

Experts don't know exactly how they learned to do what they do.

But they're usually convinced they know exactly what it takes for others to do it.

That experts cannot agree on The One True Path proves there's more than just *one* "right" way to get there. *That's encouraging.*

When experts disagree (passionately) on precisely *which* topics/ skills should be taught and in which order, they're usually missing the much bigger problem: most experts teach (and argue over) that which is easiest to *represent* rather than that which is most *valuable* for improving performance. Experts-as-teachers typically focus on knowledge and mechanics while missing the deeper core perceptual patterns and the kinds of experiences (including practice) most likely to build *real* results.

Doing the right things in the right ways makes a path robust, even if it's not the optimal path.

We want our users-as-learners to be resilient. We want them to keep moving forward *despite* problems with, say, knowledge gaps in the user manual. If their forward progress is too dependent on having access to high-quality learning materials/content and the perfect path, we risk losing them when they're struggling.

Most of the typical approaches to acquiring knowledge and skills are *fragile*. *Your* approach can be *robust*.

The secret to a motivating Path Map

It's not about the belt
It's about the progress ← this

It's about *increasing resolution*. It's about becoming *more skillful*. In martial arts, the belt is a *representation* of where you are on the path but it's also a *tool* for gaining access to new challenges, better sparring partners, richer instruction, more advanced coaching, etcetera.

It is *never* about the *belt*.
It is about what the belt *reflects* and *enables*.
It is about *meaningful progress*.

↗
This book has piles of research on the impact (and implementation) of progress indicators.

"Of all the things that can boost emotions, motivation, and perceptions during a workday, the single most important is making progress in meaningful work. And the more frequently people experience that sense of progress, the more likely they are to be creatively productive in the long run. Whether they are trying to solve a major scientific mystery or simply produce a high-quality product or service, everyday progress—even a small win—can make all the difference in how they feel and perform."
— Teresa M. Amabile, Steven J. Kramer

Exercise: design a "belt" path for your context

Compelling Context

Brainstorm around an existing path or take a first crack at designing one. Try mapping performance, results, capabilities, and skills to a color-coded belt system. If your "tool" (product, service) also has a long path to expertise, repeat this exercise for your tool.

Remember: it's about what they can do/demonstrate

Expert

Beginner

Making progress is necessary, but it's not enough

What *payoffs* are they getting along the way?

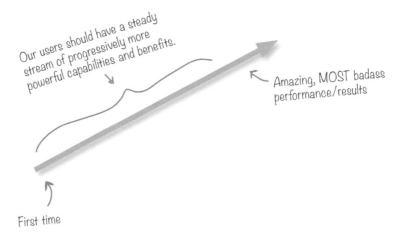

Our users should have a steady stream of progressively more powerful capabilities and benefits.

Amazing, MOST badass performance/results

First time

Helping them *believe* they'll get better matters.
Helping them *actually* get better matters.
Helping them *realize* they're getting better matters.

But none of *that* matters if they don't *benefit* from getting better.

Which brings us to...

What can they do within the first 30 minutes?

:30 minutes

**The clock is ticking...
what can he do before
the timer goes off?**

What *will* he do in the first 30 minutes?

What *could* he do in the first 30 minutes but he
doesn't know he can?

What *support* does he have in the first 30
minutes? (And does he know about it?)

What *would* he do if he knew he wouldn't
break anything?

Lower the initial threshold for user-does-something-meaningful

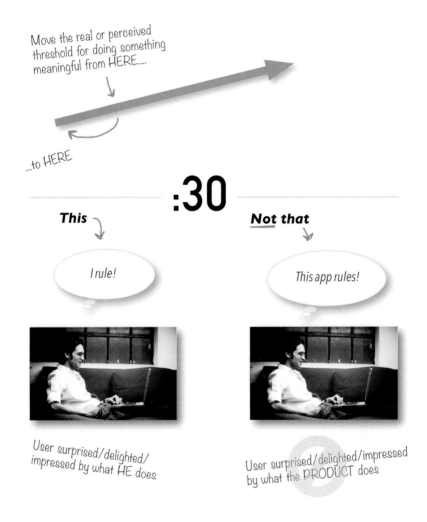

Move the real or perceived threshold for doing something meaningful from HERE....

...to HERE

:30

This

I rule!

User surprised/delighted/impressed by what HE does

Not that

This app rules!

User surprised/delighted/impressed by what the PRODUCT does

But remember *this* problem?

Before *they give us money it's all about the* **context**

After *they give us money it's just about the* **tool**

marketing → Compelling Context

"Take photos"

tool

support →

"Read the manual."

We also have *this* problem:

What they think *they can do in the first 30 minutes*:

What they actually *can do in the first 30 minutes*:

tool

"Read the manual."

Compelling Context

"Take photos"

Fear can derail them before they start

I'm afraid if I touch any settings I will NEVER get it back to the way it was.

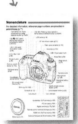

If we want them to feel powerful early, we must anticipate and compensate for anything that keeps them from experimenting.

THIS is intimidating ↓

But we can add THIS... ↓

DON'T PANIC

Recovery is easy.
Be brave.
(see inside for super
simple reset steps)

...to the manual, the quick-start guide, the product brochure, the main product page on the web, etcetera.

Convince them to be brave

Give them the freedom to
just try things.

If we want them to learn and grow and get better and stay motivated, we must give them the information and tools to recover from their experiments, and reassurance that they won't break or lose anything.

Design a Wild Experimentation Mode

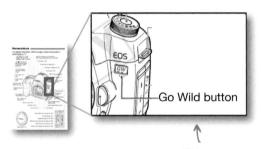

Go Wild button

THIS (imaginary) setting could help people get better faster

If we can't design Wild Experimentation Mode into our product, we *can* design it into our support by helping users feel safe and encouraged to "experiment without fear of losing how it works right now."

Meaningful with a lowercase "m"

> *This meaningful-within-30 thing works with cameras because photos are meaningful. What about all the domains where you can't do ANYTHING "meaningful" until you're much further up the curve?*

It doesn't need to be *practical* to be *meaningful.*

Remember, "meaningful-in-30-minutes" is about exceeding their expectation of what they'd be able to do at first. If within your context it's *not* possible to do anything *useful* in 30 minutes, you can still find something *meaningful.*

Surprise them with their new capability
Delight them with their own impressive result.
Inspire them to try something.

What's the smallest step they can take that leaves them feeling more creative, smart, powerful, capable?

What's the smallest step that gives a hint of *future* power?

What's the first "superpower" for your context?

What's an early small step that feels like a superpower at first?

THINK: high-payoff tips, tricks, short-cuts

Your turn. Brainstorm some small-step-big-payoff superpowers for *your* context

Don't stop after the <u>first</u> 30 minutes...

What can they do *next*? And 30 minutes after *that*? Remember, this part of our formula isn't just about *recognizing* progress, it's about *benefiting* from it.

The ideal user path is a continuous series of *loops*, each with a motivating *next superpower* goal, skill building work with exposure-to-good-examples, followed by a payoff.

Payoffs are *not* external rewards; they're the hard-earned *benefits* of effort.

Design with a motivating payoff loop

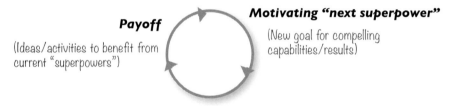

Payoff
(Ideas/activities to benefit from current "superpowers")

Motivating "next superpower"
(New goal for compelling capabilities/results)

Practice + Exposure
(Activities to build skills and knowledge)

The best payoff of all: *intrinsically rewarding experiences*

Every day we do things we would *not* do without external motivation. But the things we *truly* look forward to—that we find enjoyable and rewarding for their own sake and that we'd do without any external reward or pressure—are intrinsically motivated experiences.

The difference between extrinsically (external) vs. intrinsically motivated experiences is the difference between short-term vs. sustained motivation.

EXtrinsically rewarding   **IN**trinsically rewarding

If I do this 5 more times I get a badge

Wow... just... this is incredible. I made a fractal...

Rewarding because of an external motivator: reward, status, peer pressure, etcetera. These are NOT the payoffs that lead to robust, long-term success.

Rewarding for its own sake.

Powerful Intrinsic Motivation:
High Resolution and Flow

High Resolution

Listening

Deeper, richer experience

Appreciation for increasingly more subtle details *mere mortals* can't perceive.

Flow

Creating

"In the zone"
"In your element"

The psychology of "optimal experience" describes Flow as a state in which you're so fully absorbed in a stimulating and challenging activity that you lose sense of time.

It's the feeling experienced by rock climbers, musicians, programmers, or the passenger in seat 23C so focused on a Sudoku puzzle she didn't realize the plane was landing.

(We'll look at *Flow* in more detail in a moment.)

High-resolution: *badass users "talk different"*

Having a high-res conversation with someone who shares our knowledge, skill, and interest is a powerful intrinsically motivating experience.

> Dude, I got the new WAAS update yesterday.

> Cool. Shot an LPV approach with it yet?

> Yeah, I shot GPS 29R at LMO. Awesome stability... normally my ILSes wobble up and down a couple of dots when I get close to DH, but with this I nailed it! Crossed needles in the doughnut all the way down.

> Whoa.

Learning to understand and especially converse in the high-res technical jargon of a domain is both intrinsically rewarding and extremely useful.

You're actually SUGGESTING jargon as a GOOD thing?

Communicating with domain-specific "jargon" is both a useful tool and a stimulating reward.

What sounds like gibberish to others is meaningful and efficient communication to those who have entered the high-res world in which that jargon makes sense. Learning the technical jargon of a domain enables rich, deeply rewarding conversations and, yes, feels like a superpower. Think about how a single word of *jargon* often unpacks into something much more complex.

Don't discourage jargon use in your domain. Embrace it. Teach it. Invent it. Help your users learn it and find chances to use it.

Beginners don't necessarily hate jargon in a domain they want to join. They'd love to understand and use it ASAP. So that's our job: help beginners come up to speed on jargon, and the more they're around it, the faster that will happen. You can always create separate spaces (discussion forums) just for beginners.

If you know your beginners will be exposed to jargon, and you know they'll need some time to become fluent, *just tell them (anticipate and compensate).* Tell them their confusion is *typical* and *temporary.* The problem is not the jargon... the problem is we need to help them cope (and ultimately thrive) with it.

Flow: The psychology of optimal experience

One of the most influential books for user-experience design.

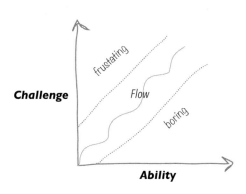

Playing a *challenging* piece that's *within* our current capability can produce an intensely motivating **Flow** experience.

The rest of the world drops away.

You *know* it when it happens, or rather, *after* it happens... "wait, it's *dark* out?"

For Flow to be possible, there must be a balance between perceived *challenge* and current *ability* to meet that challenge.

Give your users high-payoff tips

What are the simplest high-payoff tips and tricks in your domain? The earlier you help your users learn those, the quicker they'll have high-res, high-payoff, high-WOFO opportunities.

Create a web page, PDF, or video of tips and tricks, ideally grouped by level/ability. For the bigger context/domain, you can probably find an existing web-site you can recommend to your users. If you already have a user group or community site, encourage users to contribute their tricks and tips.

> *Giving "tips and tricks" is not Deliberate Practice and it's not Perceptual Exposure, so why are we doing it? Doesn't this just reinforce "mechanics without feel"?*

Remember when we said half-a-skill beats half-assed skills? We also said that when people are first starting, they need a Minimum Viable Half-Assed Skillset to be able to do something rewarding. Tips and tricks can make a motivating half-assed skill at the beginning of a curve, but they can also work at advanced levels.

This is *not* about giving people *shortcuts*; it's about helping them bypass the *unnecessarily long* way. We don't want our users to spend much time reinforcing (locking-in) beginner or mediocre skills. Tips and tricks are one way to help let users practice at being better even if they don't *yet* understand how and why the shortcut works.

Our "formula" is nearly done:

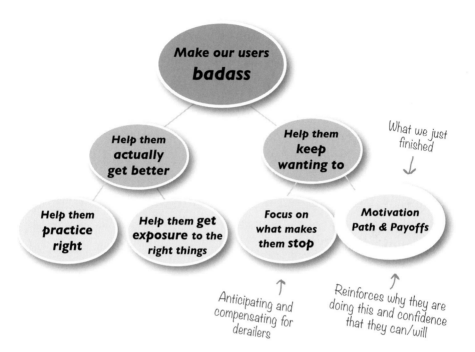

But we're missing one big thing from the formula—something that ripples through everything...

What else do we need to make it all work?

There's one more thing we need to help our users with, and it's the crucial factor in every aspect of user happiness.

It begins with an experiment...

Support Cognitive Resources
▼
Design

Small experiment, super-sized implications

In 1999, Professor Baba Shiv (currently at Stanford) and his co-author Alex Fedorikhin conducted a simple experiment with 165 grad students. They asked half to memorize a *seven*-digit number and the other half to memorize a *two*-digit number.

After completing the memorization task, participants were told the experiment was over, and then offered a snack...

...and that's when it happened.

The Experiment

1. "Memorize these numbers."

Group A	Group B
two-digit memorization task	**seven**-digit memorization task

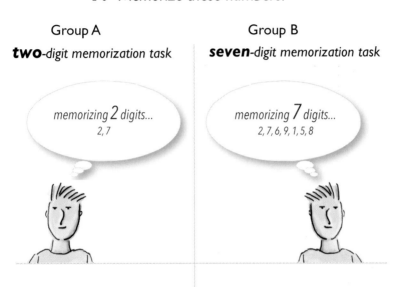

memorizing 2 digits...
2, 7

memorizing 7 digits...
2, 7, 6, 9, 1, 5, 8

2. "We're done, thank-you. Would you like a snack?"

7-digit memorizers were nearly 50% more likely to choose cake than the 2-digit memorizers.

Baba Shiv and Alex Fedorikhin, 1999

2 digits →   7 digits

The participants who memorized the seven-digit number were nearly 50% more likely than the other group to choose cake over fruit.

With this and other related experiments, the answer was more complicated than simply "brains want more calories after doing work." What researchers discovered was both counter-intuitive and stunning:

Willpower and cognitive processing draw from the same pool of resources.

The seven-digit memorizers weren't choosing cake simply because their tired brain needed more calories; *they chose cake because the memorization task depleted their willpower to resist the cake.*

Think about that.

So what you're saying is...

...that app makes me fat.

Yes.

Sort of. Maybe.

If a product you use every day is poorly-designed and hard to use, it drains your cognitive resources. That means it also drains your willpower.

NOTE: There *are* things you can do to replenish cognitive resources, but the big two are a good night's sleep and good nutrition.

There's only *one* resource pool for both willpower and cognitive tasks

Spend the morning in meetings being "polite" to people who act like THIS...

...and you might struggle to play chess in the afternoon.

Spend the day solving tricky technical problems...

...and you're more likely to hit the fast food drive-through on the way home.

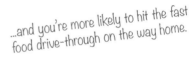  

Given what we now know about cognitive resources, it's no surprise if after a full day at work you come home and snap at the dog over something trivial.

Or the dog snaps at *you*.

The Experiment, *with dogs*

STEP ONE: "wait for <u>10 minutes</u>"

Group A *Sit obediently*	Group B *Wait in the crate*

They rigged a Tug-a-Jug toy to make it impossible for the dogs to get the treat

STEP TWO: "Here's your treat puzzle"

Gave up in
less than 1 minute

Worked on it
more than 2 minutes

Sitting obediently burned more cognitive fuel for self-control than simply waiting in the crate.

More than twice as long as the "sit" group

Common Self-Control Processes in Humans and Dogs
Holly C. Miller, Kristina F. Pattison, C. Nathan DeWall,
Rebecca Rayburn-Reeves and Thomas R. Zentall
Psychological Science April 2010.

The Challenge   What Experts Do   Help Them Move Forward   **Support Cognitive Resources**
▼
Design

Make sure your users spend their scarce, easily drained cognitive resources on the right things

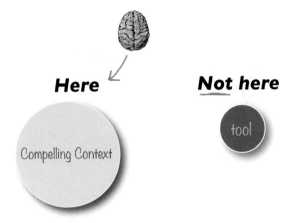

Here **Not here**

Compelling Context

tool

Think of cognitive resources as a single bank account, and every cognitive task or use of willpower as a withdrawal from that one account.

Always be asking, "where do my users want to spend their precious cognitive resources? What can we do to *help*? What are we doing that *hurts*?"

Every moment spent struggling with a confusing UI, frustrating customer service, poor documentation, or anything requiring patience, self-control, or intense concentration on the *tool* could be stealing resources from learning, practice, and becoming badass at the thing they *really* care about: *the context.*

Cognitive resource management for your users is mainly about reducing leaks

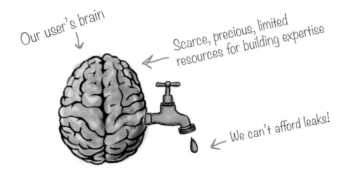

Our user's brain

Scarce, precious, limited resources for building expertise

We can't afford leaks!

Becoming badass is hard.
There will be cognitive resource drain.

You **do** want your users to *use* cognitive resources.

You **don't** want your users to *waste* them.

Don't make them think about the wrong things.

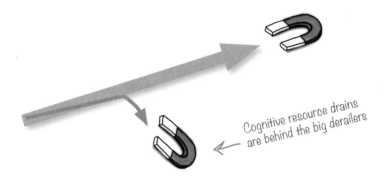

Cognitive resource drains are behind the big derailers

Zeigarnik Effect leaks
(and why anticipate-and-compensate helps)

The Zeigarnik Effect, named after the late Soviet psychologist Bluma Zeigarnik, suggests that the brain keeps a background process running for unfinished/interrupted tasks. Novelists and filmmakers *depend* on the cognitive tension caused by unresolved plot elements and cliffhangers to keep you turning the pages or waiting for the next episode. It's not just *you* (the *conscious* you) that's dying to know how it all turns out—it's also your *brain* that can't let it go.

The Zeigarnik Effect means cognitive resources are being consumed in the background while you're doing other things. The more open/unfinished tasks that are running in the background, the less resources are available for focusing, practicing, and learning.

What if you DO accidentally unplug it? That could TOTALLY happen but they don't talk about it...

I'm not letting this go. I'll just keep an open thread running in the background until it's resolved. Carry on.

leads to

Your brain keeps track of an unresolved cognitive task, long after "you" stop thinking about it. That slow background leak is the Zeigarnik Effect in action.

Your brain won't need to spend resources "worrying" about an unfinished cognitive task if it "believes" something or someone has a trustworthy plan for handling it.

What if the alarm doesn't go off? OMG you CAN'T oversleep and miss that flight. Maybe I should just keep you awake all night to be safe.

Between my phone alarm and the Clocky, there is NO WAY I'll oversleep.

I got this. I'll roll off the night-stand and across the room until you shut me off.

The Clocky alarm clock forces you out of bed to turn it off.

Ok, so that's handled...

Even though the unfinished task (waking up on time) has not actually been resolved, knowing that the "job" has been delegated to trustable alarms is enough for the brain to act as if it's already been handled.

Death by a thousand cognitive microleaks

Designer Dan Saffer describes
microinteractions as "contained product
moments that revolve around a single
use case—they have one main task." His
book *Microinteractions* covers how to
design microinteractions in a way that
doesn't just close cognitive leaks but brings
"personality and delight" to apps and
devices.

A common cognitive microleak comes
from that subtle feeling of uncertainty
about whether some small action you took
did exactly what you intended.

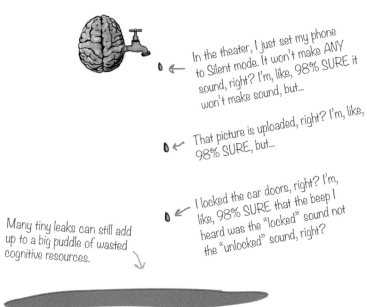

In the theater, I just set my phone
to Silent mode. It won't make ANY
sound, right? I'm, like, 98% SURE it
won't make sound, but...

That picture is uploaded, right? I'm, like,
98% SURE, but...

I locked the car doors, right? I'm,
like, 98% SURE that the beep I
heard was the "locked" sound not
the "unlocked" sound, right?

Many tiny leaks can still add
up to a big puddle of wasted
cognitive resources.

When you're considering adding a new feature...

"is this a cake feature or a fruit feature?"

Does this feature drain their cognitive resources?

Is this feature *worth* the drain?

Does this feature directly contribute to user expertise and results for the meaningful bigger context?

Is there a way to hide or minimize the feature until the user is ready for it?

Remember, cognitive leaks are cumulative (memorizing *one* digit was no problem, but *seven* drained the tank!). Even if *this* feature is itself a "fruit-choosing" (low cognitive task), in the context of other features, it might be one too many.

Support Cognitive Resources
▼
Design ►**Reduce Cognitive Leaks**

To reduce their cognitive leaks, delegate cognitive work to something in the *world*
(so it doesn't have to be in the user's *head*)

I have to set-up the stereo

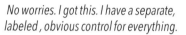
No worries. I got this. I have a separate, labeled, obvious control for everything.

Delegates to

Knowledge for using it is in the *world*
(the device itself)

I have to set-up the stereo

Dude. Read my manual. Then admire my sleek, elegant interface, without all those clunky controls or *words* cluttering up the front. You'll figure it out... eventually.

Tries to delegate

delegation FAIL

Knowledge for using it must be in the user's *head*
(because it's *not* in the device)

The Challenge   What Experts Do   Help Them Move Forward   ***Support Cognitive Resources***
▼
Design   ▶**Reduce Cognitive Leaks**

229

Don't make them memorize

Always be asking: "Do they *really* need to remember this or can we stick it in a cheat sheet or put a better label on the button?" Does this knowledge *really* need to be in their head?

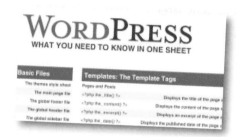

Cheat sheets save users from spending cognitive resources trying to memorize and recall, especially with tasks they don't do frequently.

Most manuals are not usable enough to compensate for a bad user interface. Knowledge in the *manual* is not the same as knowledge in the *world*. If they have to consult the manual more than once for the same task, that's draining the user's cognitive resources.

The Challenge   What Experts Do   Help Them Move Forward   **Support Cognitive Resources**
▼
Design   ▶**Reduce Cognitive Leaks**

230

Knowledge in the head vs. world is a trade-off

Learning and memorizing drains cognitive resources, but after you've learned/memorized it, using the now-automatic/memorized knowledge and skill is fast and effortless. Knowledge in the head trades slower learning/using time now for faster using time later.

For both your bigger context and your tool, tell your users *which* facts and procedures are worth spending the effort to memorize, and *when* they should do it.

*"It's not necessary or worth it to memorize **those** right now, so here's where to look them up when you need them. But when you start doing* [more advanced thing]*, it'll make life easier if you spend a few days memorizing **these**...."*

The concept of "knowledge in the head vs. knowledge in the world" was popularized by Donald Norman, in *The Design of Everyday Things*. If you can choose just *one* book about design, UI, usability, saving cognitive resources, and caring about users—*this is that book.*

The power of *affordances*: to reduce their cognitive leaks, make the *right* thing to do the most *likely* thing to do

naturally "pushable"

obviously "pullable"

The more obvious/self-evident it is to take Action A vs. Action B, the fewer cognitive resources we use for that action. Product designers often refer to this as "perceived affordances," popularized by Donald Norman in *The Design of Everyday Things* (the same book that popularized "knowledge in the *head* vs. *world*").

A natural, obvious, self-evident action can be a perceived affordance, an instinctive reaction, or simply the easiest path of least resistance.

> *"Make the right thing easy and the wrong thing difficult."*
>
> —horse trainer mantra

The Challenge   What Experts Do   Help Them Move Forward   **Support Cognitive Resources**
▼
Design   ▶**Reduce Cognitive Leaks**

232

To reduce their cognitive leaks, make the *right* action the most *natural and obvious* action

Looks... looks... pullable? Or is it pushable...

For every action your users need to take (and for every new feature you're considering), ask yourself, "What's the most likely thing to do here?" If the most likely action is *not* the right action, you might need to add knowledge in the *world* to help. But afordances are powerful—we've all experienced *pulling* a door handle labeled PUSH simply because it *looked* pullable.

When the action to take is not instantly obvious/natural, we're forced to look for other cues or use trial-and-error.

Naturally "pushable" does NOT invite you to grasp and pull

This was meant to be PUSHED, but it's not instantly obvious and natural, and unlike the previous picture, THESE look like handles meant to be grasped.

Obviously "pullable"

The Challenge   What Experts Do   Help Them Move Forward   **Support Cognitive Resources**
                                                                        ▼
                                          Design   ▶**Reduce Cognitive Leaks**

233

To reduce their cognitive leaks, don't make them choose

Choices are cognitively expensive

How our users feel about having lots of options

What we THINK   What's actually TRUE

I have so much more control! I have choices for everything. I feel so autonomous and powerful and awesome.

I can't feel my legs...

What they ACTUALLY feel LATER

Choices aren't just cognitively costly *while* we're choosing, they drain cognitive resources *after* we choose.

Wait... did I make the right choice? Maybe I should have.. I just...

Leaving the decision to someone else saves the cognitive expense of deciding and frees us from the cognitive drain of second-guessing ourselves later.

The Challenge   What Experts Do   Help Them Move Forward   **Support Cognitive Resources**
▼
Design   ▶**Reduce Cognitive Leaks**

234

There's a world of difference between *having* choices and having to *make* choices.

Choices give us more control and a more customized experience, but it comes at a cost. Think about times when you were relieved to have someone else make the choice.

In the perfect scenario, we give our users as many options as they could want or need, but we also give them trusted defaults, pre-sets, and recommendations. Especially in the beginning, we make decisions so our users don't have to.

Be the expert, the mentor, the guide.

Be the one who says, "Trust me, based on what you want to do and where you are now, *this* is what you should choose."

The Challenge   *What Experts Do*   *Help Them Move Forward*   ***Support Cognitive Resources***
                                                               ▼
                                            Design   ▶**Reduce Cognitive Leaks**

235

To reduce their cognitive leaks, help them *automate skills*

Skills in "B" drain cognitive resources. "C" skills are cognitively cheap.

Remember, the single biggest problem for most people learning a complex skill is working on too many sub-skills simultaneously instead of nailing one sub-skill at a time.

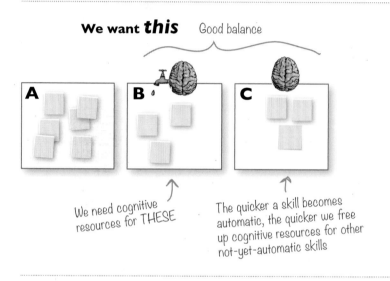

We want *this* Good balance

A B C

We need cognitive resources for THESE

The quicker a skill becomes automatic, the quicker we free up cognitive resources for other not-yet-automatic skills

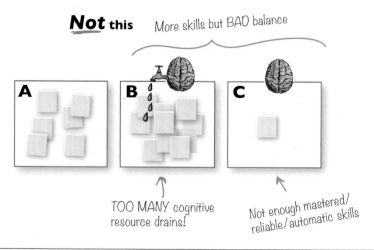

***Not* this** More skills but BAD balance

A B C

TOO MANY cognitive resource drains!

Not enough mastered/ reliable/ automatic skills

*The Challenge   What Experts Do   Help Them Move Forward   **Support Cognitive Resources***
▼
Design   ▶**Reduce Cognitive Leaks**

236

To reduce their cognitive leaks, give them practice hacks

Deliberate Practice drains cognitive resources. Help your users make everything else <u>around</u> practice easier to do.

Give your users ideas and templates for tracking and logging using a practice notebook. Field Notes work well for this.

Design or recommend a practice notebook

Design a physical notebook to track progress and log each practice session. Give your users ideas, tips, tricks for how to design their own notebook tracking system, including charts and graphs to show progress over time.

Another practice hack is to log cognitive resources and physical energy. The more you know about when you're in the best physical and mental state for practice, the more you can optimize and organize your practice sessions.

Lift is a simple, free motivation/goal tracking app.

Design or recommend tracking apps

The availability of social media software (and communities) to track progress is a mixed blessing. Community sites can support and encourage practice and sustained motivation, but they can also drain cognitive resources.

Help your users find and use a tracking app (and community) that doesn't try to suck people into spending time on the site. One example is Lift, which provides a simple way for your users to track whether they did a specific habit/practice each day. Lift also lets you create a group with specific practice goals just for your users.

The Challenge   *What Experts Do*   *Help Them Move Forward*   ***Support Cognitive Resources***
▼
Design   ▶**Reduce Cognitive Leaks**

237

To reduce their cognitive leaks, help with the top-of-mind problem

For consistent, repeating reminders

Some skills can't be improved much using only Deliberate Practice. What happens when you want to improve your *posture?* Or remember to make *eye contact?* Or *breathe* better? Or fix a *speech pattern?* In other words, what if the problem is not lack of skill but lack of constant reminders? Fortunately there's a simple, powerful tool for solving the massively-draining top-of-mind problem: the MotivAider.

If you're trying to change your posture, how do you constantly remind yourself to "sit straight"?

Repeating reminder device (also available as a phone app)

I don't care if it's annoying, How many times do I have to remind you to stand up straight? Shoulders back!

Replace THIS...

...with THIS

"Helpful" person

MotivAider is a wearable device that gives silent (vibrating) repeating reminders at consistent intervals from one *minute* to many *hours.* It's designed for keeping something at the top of your mind, *without draining cognitive resources.*

MotivAider also helps with cognitive resources during Deliberate Practice

Imagine you're practicing piano, focusing all your cognitive resources on what you're playing, and you're *also* trying to remember to relax the tension in your upper back. But you can't do both simultaneously.

Now imagine you put the MotivAider in your pocket and set the timer for two minute intervals. Every two minutes, as you're playing, you'll feel a gentle, subtle momentary vibration which works as a reminder for you to relax the tension in your back. The power of the device (as opposed to the app) is this: the vibration is tuned to be just enough for your brain to notice the "trigger" without taking you out of what you're actually working on. Think about that.

Trying to keep thing A at top-of-mind while simultaneously working on thing B is a background drain. Worse, it doesn't work. You can't keep reminding yourself over and over while working on tasks that demand cognitive attention.

Tell your users about the MotivAider! Give them tips for ways to use it to get better at your context. Encourage users to share their top-of-mind problems. It's like a superpower.

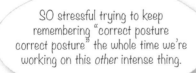
SO stressful trying to keep remembering "correct posture correct posture" the whole time we're working on this *other* intense thing.

No worries. I got this.

The Challenge   What Experts Do   Help Them Move Forward   **Support Cognitive Resources**
▼
Design   ▶**Reduce Cognitive Leaks**

239

To reduce their cognitive leaks, reduce the need for willpower

Self-control / willpower is cognitively expensive

Memorized 2 numbers, chose fruit

Memorized 7 numbers, chose cake

The harder cognitive task depleted the willpower tank because, remember, it's all the same tank.

Our users need cognitive resources to do the hard mental and physical work of getting better, but they also need willpower for doing the hard things. And remember, willpower and cognitive processing draw from the same pool of resources.

We talked about helping our users stay motivated, but no matter how much they want to practice and study and get better, if they don't have enough cognitive resources they won't be able to do the tedious or difficult things. Not because they aren't motivated, but because their cognitive resource tank is drained.

Remember, half of the "seven digits" memorizers *would* have chosen fruit but their self-control was drained by those extra five digits. Just *five* extra digits was enough to dent their willpower.

The secret to **willpower** is... *assume it doesn't exist*

Imagine you wake up in the hospital following a car accident and the doctor describes your condition...

The *good* news is your *leg* will be fine. Simple tibia break, cast comes off in a month.

Whew! What's the *bad* news?

I'm afraid the damage to your *willpower* was irreparable. It's... it's *gone*.

What would you do?

What would you do if your willpower was surgically removed?

Every moment you're using willpower means fewer resources for thinking, learning, and practice. Every moment you're doing difficult learning and practice means fewer resources for willpower.

And *that's* without considering all the ways in which the *rest* of your daily life drains your cognitive resources.

Take a moment to imagine what changes you would make to your life if you could no longer depend on willpower.

Those things you would do if your willpower was surgically removed?

Do them for your users.

BRAND X
New Formula!

Willpower Not Required!

*The Challenge   What Experts Do   Help Them Move Forward   **Support Cognitive Resources***
▼
Design ▶**Reduce Cognitive Leaks**

242

To reduce the need for willpower, help them build automatic habits

Habits require little or no willpower. Think of all the behaviors your users need to have on their path to badass, and find ways to help them develop habits *around* those behaviors.

Seriously? Just when the light is perfect there's only two minutes of battery left? And the memory card is full?

Deliberate practice activities will *never* be a habit (they *require* conscious effort), but many things *around* practice can be. Habits are a crucial part of building expertise, but it's not just about creating *new* habits. We also have to upgrade or replace the *bad* habits that lead to plateaus and stuck-in-intermediate blues.

If your bigger context is photography, what are the behaviors your aspiring photographer/user must do?

Take photos ⟵ CAN'T be automatic...

Charging batteries
Importing photos from card to computer
Keeping memory cards empty/ready

...but things that support it can be

Actual *shooting* can't—and shouldn't—be automatic, but many of the supporting behaviors around shooting photos can be.

You can learn to help users build habits by reading Charles Duhigg's book, *The Power of Habit*. (And get your users to read it, too)

The Challenge   *What Experts Do*   *Help Them Move Forward*   ***Support Cognitive Resources***
                                                    ▼
                                          Design   ▶**Reduce Cognitive Leaks**

243

To reduce the need for willpower help them have intrinsically rewarding experiences

Remember, "intrinsically rewarding" means "rewarding to do for its own sake."

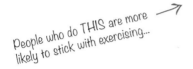
People who do THIS are more likely to stick with exercising...

...than people who just do THAT →

The more skillful we are and the higher our resolution, the more intrinsically rewarding experiences we have within a specific domain. Intrinsically motivating experiences don't require willpower because we *want* to do them. We *love* doing them.

Remember from the "help them move forward" section of the book: intrinsically rewarding experiences are the ultimate payoff for making progress. They're the reason we're willing to do the hard *non*-intrinsically-rewarding work.

*The Challenge   What Experts Do   Help Them Move Forward   **Support Cognitive Resources***
▼
Design   ▶**Reduce Cognitive Leaks**

244

> *Big problem: Deliberate Practice is NOT intrinsically rewarding. They'll still need willpower for doing the hard work.*

Actually, there is a way that some of the hard, non-intrinsically-rewarding activities can be nearly as motivating as the ones we do enjoy.

Though he does NOT enjoy running, he doesn't need as much willpower to do THIS...

↓

...because it's part of being badass at THIS

↙

"I run because I am a rock climber."

(Of course what person A finds intrinsically rewarding might be painful, hard, unrewarding effort for person B. Running, for example, is enjoyable in the moment for some but for others, it's rewarding *only when it's over.*)

The Challenge   *What Experts Do*   *Help Them Move Forward*   ***Support Cognitive Resources***
▼
Design   ▶**Reduce Cognitive Leaks**

245

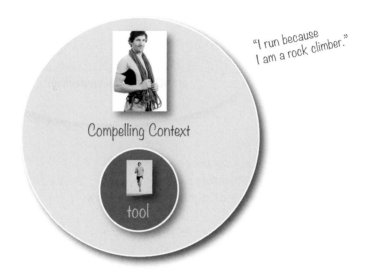

"I run because I am a rock climber."

Compelling Context

tool

When the bigger context is not just something you *do* but something you *are*, motivation for the non-enjoyable parts takes less willpower

When that happens, your relationship to the required but *non*-intrinsically rewarding work changes. In terms of *willpower demand*, some of the *non*-pleasurable work can be indistinguishable from the deeply rewarding experiences that take little or no willpower. The work is still just as hard, painful, frustrating, and *non*-rewarding—the activities don't magically *become* pleasurable—but they *do* become less dependent on willpower.

When the bigger context is part of your identity, the hard-but-necessary work becomes nearly just as motivating as the intrinsically rewarding experiences.

The Challenge *What Experts Do* *Help Them Move Forward* ***Support Cognitive Resources***
▼
Design ▶**Reduce Cognitive Leaks**

246

> *Aren't we missing the TOTALLY OBVIOUS? Why not just give them EXtrinsic rewards for the parts that are NOT INtrinsically rewarding?*

Obvious? Yes.
Intuitively good idea? Yes.

Actually good idea? No.

Motivation... *it's complicated.*
It's not as simple as intrinsic vs. extrinsic.

Giving extrinsic rewards for anything we hope to sustain long-term can do more harm than good. Extrinsic rewards are especially dangerous because they often *are* motivating in the beginning. But it's motivation around the *reward*, not motivation for the activity we hope will be rewarding for its *own* sake.

Read "Drive" by Dan Pink for a better understanding of the subtle and surprising science of motivation.

Extrinsic rewards are almost never a good answer for getting people to do that which is not yet — but could be — rewarding on its own. If we want to reward users without the long-term negative side effects, we can make the rewards completely unexpected, not directly tied to the users' behavior. For example, a special thank-you gift is a powerful "reward" without the harmful side effects.

*The Challenge   What Experts Do   Help Them Move Forward   **Support Cognitive Resources***
▼
Design   ▶**Reduce Cognitive Leaks**

247

To reduce the need for willpower, help their brain pay attention

Staying focused takes self-control

Make paying attention easier.

You've been there: you're reading a dry textbook or journal article, and there's a lot at stake. Maybe it's tomorrow's exam or that crucial presentation. And yet... you just... can't.... focus. You're reading the same page over and over. You fall asleep. You're distracted by the subtlest change in noise or light.

You and your brain are in an epic battle over what really matters.

> I really REALLY need to learn this.

> This is SO not life-threatening. Can't. Stay. Awake.... **Pizza? Do I smell pizza?!**

What WE think

What our BRAIN thinks

The Challenge   *What Experts Do*   *Help Them Move Forward*   **Support Cognitive Resources**
▼
Design   ▶**Reduce Cognitive Leaks**

248

Get past the brain's spam filter

Our brain works hard to separate signal from noise, which would be wonderful except *we* don't get to control that spam filter. Not directly, anyway. We need a way to stop the brain from treating what we care about as useless spam. To help our users pay attention and stay focused, help *their* brain realize, "This matters! **Not spam!** *Let it through!*"

Of all the things the brain *could* pay attention to at any moment...

...only a few make it past the filter

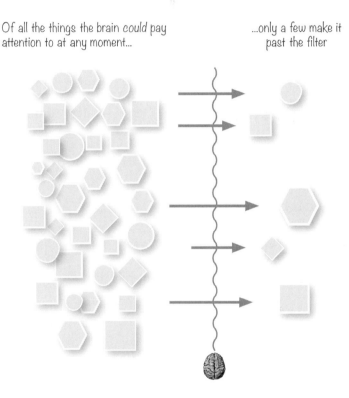

Dry, dull, emotionally lifeless content is spam to the brain. To get past the filter, the brain must agree that yes, this matters!

How do you get past the brain's spam filter?

We *must* give the brain a reason to "care"

...and that would be...

Support Cognitive Resources
▼
Design ▶Reduce Cognitive Leaks ▶**Escape the Brain's Spam Filter**

We must help our user's *brain* agree:

This is something to *care about.*

This is something to *pay attention to.*

This is something to *remember.*

Ooooh I felt that. Wow, look at THAT. Wait, this is so strange. Ouch! I better remember THAT.

Wherever staying focused is something our user wants and needs but struggles to do, we must help convince their brain to agree.

We must inject the thing our user wants to do with something our user's brain cares about.

Then what _do_ brains care about?

The Challenge   *What Experts Do*   *Help Them Move Forward*   ***Support Cognitive Resources***
▼
Design   ▶Reduce Cognitive Leaks   ▶**Escape the Brain's Spam Filter**

252

Brains care about scary, threatening things.

The Challenge   What Experts Do   Help Them Move Forward   ***Support Cognitive Resources***
▼
Design   ▶Reduce Cognitive Leaks   ▶**Escape the Brain's Spam Filter**

253

Brains care about faces, especially those showing strong emotion.

The Challenge   *What Experts Do*   *Help Them Move Forward*   ***Support Cognitive Resources***
▼
Design   ▶Reduce Cognitive Leaks   ▶**Escape the Brain's Spam Filter**

254

:)

Not just HUMAN faces.

*The Challenge   What Experts Do   Help Them Move Forward   **Support Cognitive Resources***
▼
Design ▶Reduce Cognitive Leaks **▶Escape the Brain's Spam Filter**

255

Brains care about young, helpless, things.

The Challenge   *What Experts Do*   *Help Them Move Forward*   ***Support Cognitive Resources***
▼
Design   ▶Reduce Cognitive Leaks   ▶**Escape the Brain's Spam Filter**

256

> I'm sensing a chemical surge.
> Could be joy. I better tag this thing
> as "possibly important."

Brains care about things that cause a feeling. Even if your brain has no idea why you find that thing funny, it finds your emotional response (even a subtle one) reason enough to get past the spam filter.

The Challenge   What Experts Do   Help Them Move Forward   **Support Cognitive Resources**
                                        ▼
                        Design   ▶Reduce Cognitive Leaks   ▶**Escape the Brain's Spam Filter**

257

Brains pay attention to things that
are odd, surprising, unexpected.

The Challenge   What Experts Do   Help Them Move Forward   **Support Cognitive Resources**
▼
Design   ▶Reduce Cognitive Leaks   ▶**Escape the Brain's Spam Filter**

258

Brains want things resolved. What happens next?
Brains want the answer.

The Zeigarnik Effect drains cognitive resources, but we can also use the Zeigarnik Effect strategically, like a filmmaker, to keep the brain interested.

The Challenge   *What Experts Do*   *Help Them Move Forward*   ***Support Cognitive Resources***
▼
Design   ▶Reduce Cognitive Leaks   ▶**Escape the Brain's Spam Filter**

259

How am I supposed to actually USE this to make something more attention-grabby? I can't just shove a pile of gratuitous puppy pictures on everything...

Actually you *could* put gratuitous puppy pictures on every otherwise *non*-attention-grabby thing your users need to focus on. And it could work. At first.

Remember, the brain cares about things it does *not* expect. Once your puppy photos have become expected, the brain stops noticing them and they might as well be dull, dry text. Fodder for the spam folder.

We don't need to use *photos* to get the brain's attention, but we need some way to provoke a feeling. Always be asking, "What can we do to make the brain care about this? How can we create a feeling?"

Even the most subtle feeling is better than emotional flatline.

← Gratuitous puppy picture

*The Challenge   What Experts Do   Help Them Move Forward   **Support Cognitive Resources***
▼
Design   ▶Reduce Cognitive Leaks   ▶**Escape the Brain's Spam Filter**

260

Make it visceral

Getting the brain's attention through a captivating, useful, visceral example, picture, or story saves resources and increases memorability (for the things they MUST memorize).

Though you *could* get their attention with something totally unrelated to what they're trying to learn, it's far better for learning and retention if the *feeling* you evoke to get their attention is about what you want them to remember.

Example: teaching software design patterns

To a programmer, the diagram below creates an instant, implicit feeling of dread. We *could* tell them with words alone, "this design approach can lead to problems..." Using words alone, the user/learner would understand it *technically*, but is that enough for their brain to care?

Rather than *telling* our user/learner what a specific (bad) design could lead to, *showing* them the resulting horror grabs the brain by the throat.

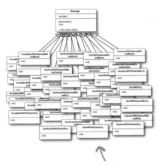

To a programmer, this diagram
inspires a feeling of horror...

I'm **never** making the mistake
that led to *that* disaster.
Never. OMG.

Make it visceral to get
the brain's attention *and*
improve memorability

The Challenge   *What Experts Do*   *Help Them Move Forward*   ***Support Cognitive Resources***
▼
Design   ▶Reduce Cognitive Leaks   ▶**Escape the Brain's Spam Filter**

261

Convince their brain with *context*

Most marketing content is more learnable and memorable than most learning content. The difference in production values between marketing vs. a user manual is not what matters most. The key difference? Marketing is about the *context*; manuals are about the *tool*.

From the brain's POV:

it's all about the context

marketing → Compelling Context

Stimulating, easy to understand, keeps your attention, focuses on what you really want to do, improves learning and memory.

Putting it in a compelling context helps give it a pulse.

it's just about the tool

tool

support →

Dry, hard to read, and organized around functions of the tool, NOT why you'd want to use them. NOT learner/brain friendly.

Trying to learn something with an emotional flatline.

The Challenge   *What Experts Do*   *Help Them Move Forward*   ***Support Cognitive Resources***
▼
Design   ▶Reduce Cognitive Leaks   ▶**Escape the Brain's Spam Filter**

262

Use "Why? So what? Who cares?"

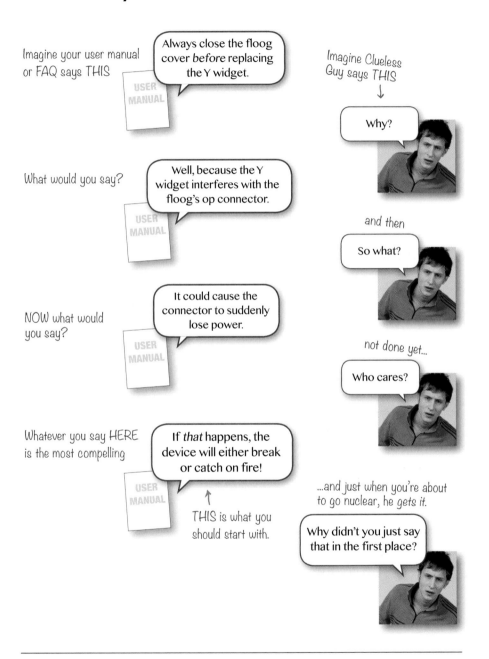

Imagine your user manual or FAQ says THIS

> Always close the floog cover *before* replacing the Y widget.

USER MANUAL

What would you say?

> Well, because the Y widget interferes with the floog's op connector.

USER MANUAL

NOW what would you say?

> It could cause the connector to suddenly lose power.

USER MANUAL

Whatever you say HERE is the most compelling

> If *that* happens, the device will either break or catch on fire!

USER MANUAL

↑ THIS is what you should start with.

Imagine Clueless Guy says THIS
↓

> Why?

and then

> So what?

not done yet...

> Who cares?

...and just when you're about to go nuclear, he *gets it*.

> Why didn't you just say that in the first place?

The Challenge   What Experts Do   Help Them Move Forward   **Support Cognitive Resources**
▼
Design   ▶Reduce Cognitive Leaks   ▶**Escape the Brain's Spam Filter**

263

Brains don't want to waste scarce resources making those "little" leaps

Remember, this isn't about your users' *intelligence*, it's about their brain's *spam filter*. Yes, they could make the leap... *if their brain were already riveted.*

You've experienced this while reading a textbook or user manual: you read clear, straightforward paragraph after paragraph, page after page, thinking OK, makes sense, yes, whatever, and then at the end BAM! Suddenly there's *this* sentence, "If you forget to do this, here's the [catastrophic thing] that will happen..."

That warning is way too late.

Note: Sometimes we *do* want *them* to make the logical leaps, but that means specifically designing a context to lead them into deeper thinking.

The Challenge   What Experts Do   Help Them Move Forward   ***Support Cognitive Resources***
▼
Design   ▶Reduce Cognitive Leaks   ▶**Escape the Brain's Spam Filter**

264

The best way to deal with the brain's spam filter is to reduce the amount of things that need to get past it

Making content *easier* for their brain to pay attention to is good. Making *less* content for their brain to pay attention to is much better.

Does that knowledge *really* need to be in the manual?

Do they *really* need to read the "knowledge base" articles on the web-site?

Do they *really* need to read the *whole* book we recommended before they get started or can they read just the first two chapters for now?

Do they *really* need to participate in that webinar?

The Challenge   What Experts Do   Help Them Move Forward   **Support Cognitive Resources**
▼
Design   ▶Reduce Cognitive Leaks   ▶**Escape the Brain's Spam Filter**

265

What about the facts they absolutely positively *must* know?

> *They can't just practice and build skills. They do need to learn, you know, ACTUAL FACTS.*

Yes, yes they do.

But the best time for explicit knowledge is *only when absolutely needed.*

Remember this diagram?

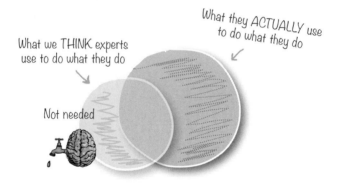

What we THINK experts use to do what they do

What they ACTUALLY use to do what they do

Not needed

We can't afford to waste scarce resources on facts and procedures *before* they're needed.

The Challenge   *What Experts Do*   *Help Them Move Forward*   ***Support Cognitive Resources***
▼
Design   ▶Reduce Cognitive Leaks   ▶**Escape the Brain's Spam Filter**

266

Brains prefer Just-in-*Time* over Just-in-*Case*

Trying to learn knowledge before you need to use it
(Just-in-Case) means fighting the spam filter

Just-In-*Time* means learning something only when/because you
actually need to use it. But Just-In-*Case* is the predominant
model for most forms of education (and most user manuals).
Just-in-*Case* knowledge is easier to present, but harder to learn,
understand, and remember. Much harder.

To the brain, Just-in-*Case* can seem useless.

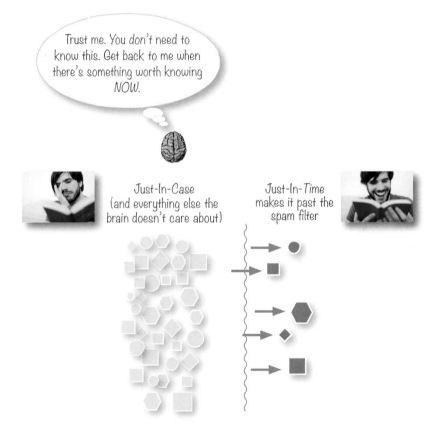

Trust me. You *don't* need to know this. Get back to me when there's something worth knowing NOW.

Just-In-Case
(and everything else the
brain doesn't care about)

Just-In-Time
makes it past the
spam filter

The Challenge   What Experts Do   Help Them Move Forward   ***Support Cognitive Resources***
▼
Design   ▶Reduce Cognitive Leaks   ▶**Escape the Brain's Spam Filter**

267

Pretty sure I don't want my neurosurgeon doing "Just-In-Time" learning.

Obviously not everything can (or should) be learned Just-in-Time. But most learning in most contexts has way too much Just-in-Case. Unnecessary knowledge acquisition slows our progress. It drains our scarce time and cognitive resources. And chances are, by the time we finally *need* that knowledge to do something, we can't remember it.

Our brain filters not just what we pay attention *now* but also what we can later *remember*. From our brain's POV, why waste energy building memories of... spam? If our *brain's* not convinced the Just-in-Time knowledge matters, it will "helpfully" save us the cognitive expense of *recording* it.

But if there *is* Just-in-Case knowledge your users absolutely *must* learn *before* they need to use it, minimize the damage:

1. Validate
Are you really really *really* certain they **must** know this **right now?**

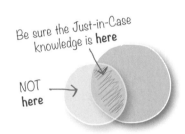

Be sure the Just-in-Case knowledge is **here**

NOT → here

2. Convince their brain
Now that *you're* sure users *must* learn this Just-in-Case knowledge, you have to "sell" it to their *brain*.

I'll give you 30 seconds to convince me. GO.

The Challenge   What Experts Do   Help Them Move Forward   **Support Cognitive Resources**
▼
Design   ▶Reduce Cognitive Leaks   ▶**Escape the Brain's Spam Filter**

268

Validate the need for this knowledge

Our job is to help filter what our users *must* learn. Our job is to help them make progress, not just *know* more.

What knowledge goes on the board?

don't know (but need to)	Can apply and recall **with effort**	Use and recall is **automatic**

A

B

C

Of all the facts, procedures, concepts, they *could* know, what goes on the A board, and when does it go there?

Even if *you're* not the one teaching (or making available) the knowledge your users need for the bigger context, help them figure out what matters *now* and what to ignore or postpone.

From a badass users POV, we're responsible for creating an expertise path for our users, regardless of where and from whom they're getting their learning content/experiences.

The first step is to narrow down the topics. We'll use two approaches to validate the knowledge our users are expected to learn: topics on trial, and mapping to skills.

*The Challenge   What Experts Do   Help Them Move Forward   **Support Cognitive Resources***
▼
Design   ▶Reduce Cognitive Leaks   ▶**Escape the Brain's Spam Filter**

269

To cut resource-draining Just-in-Case knowledge:
put each topic on trial

Interrogate each topic. Make it plead for a coveted slot on the A board. Try the Why/So What/ Who Cares game on every topic, sub-topic, fact, procedure... *everything* they're asked to learn.

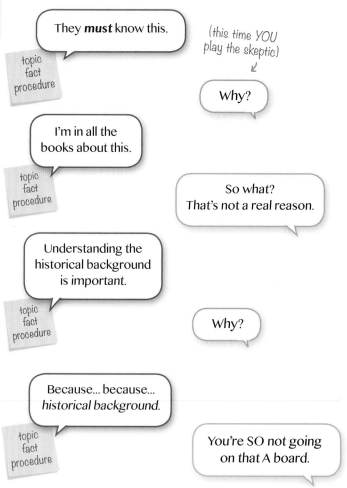

They **must** know this.

topic
fact
procedure

(this time YOU play the skeptic)

Why?

I'm in all the books about this.

topic
fact
procedure

So what?
That's not a real reason.

Understanding the historical background is important.

topic
fact
procedure

Why?

Because... because... *historical background.*

topic
fact
procedure

You're SO not going on that A board.

The Challenge   What Experts Do   Help Them Move Forward   ***Support Cognitive Resources***
▼
Design   ▶Reduce Cognitive Leaks   ▶**Escape the Brain's Spam Filter**

270

Validate knowledge usefulness by mapping it to skills

We can validate (and reduce) the knowledge they *must* learn by mapping each thing on a Knowledge board to something on a Skills board.

Knowledge *board*

Skills *board*

don't know

can't do (but need to)

1 Compile the cards of initial knowledge and skills

2 Map the knowledge to a skill and verify that you can't *possibly* do this skill without this knowledge

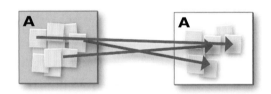

3 Remove orphaned (unmapped) knowledge. But just to be sure, check the Skills board to see if you're missing a skill that *should* be there—a skill that your unmapped knowledge *does* support. But be brave. Cut needless knowledge. Never forget cognitive resources are scarce and limited.

Unmapped Knowledge cards could mean a Skill card is missing but we're far more likely to find extraneous Knowledge than missing Skills.

So we're dissing "intellectual curiosity" as a valid reason? Must EVERYTHING be judged purely on its "utility"? What about high-res?

Be brutal.
Be brave.
Cut Cut Cut.

Knowledge cards that are *not* mapped to a Skill card should be *exceptions*. Exceptions you make very *very* rarely.

Obviously there *are* exceptions. Maybe your user/learner needs to know something to satisfy someone *else*. Or perhaps the not-necessary-but-valuable knowledge is intrinsically *fascinating* and adds high-resolution to the experience.

But there's a misconception about *intellectual curiosity*...

The Challenge   What Experts Do   Help Them Move Forward   ***Support Cognitive Resources***
                                                                    ▼
                    Design   ▶Reduce Cognitive Leaks   ▶**Escape the Brain's Spam Filter**

272

The problem with "intellectual curiosity"

Yes, our users do (or will) have intellectual curiosity around the domain. The better they become, the more interest they have for deeper historical context, origin stories, key people, side-trips, and so on. But in the beginning?

Cognitive resources. Scarce. Limited. **Zero sum.** The problem is not *if* they're intellectually curious, it's *when*.

(In books or user guides, an appendix is a useful compromise for including non-necessary-but-interesting knowledge. Users who want it will find it, but overwhelmed users won't feel pressured to learn it.)

The history of the internet is fascinating and will obviously enrich my ability to begin learning to appreciate and one day actually hope to create digital graphics...

← What we THINK they're feeling

What they're ACTUALLY feeling
↓

---

*The Challenge   What Experts Do   Help Them Move Forward   **Support Cognitive Resources***
▼
Design   ▶Reduce Cognitive Leaks   ▶**Escape the Brain's Spam Filter**

273

Speaking of limited cognitive resources (mine), we've come a looooong way in making "the formula": help users build expertise, help them stay motivated to make progress, and especially, help conserve their cognitive resources by reducing cognitive leaks.

I know what I have to do.

That's good, because...

The Challenge   What Experts Do   Help Them Move Forward   **Support Cognitive Resources**
▼
Design   ▶Reduce Cognitive Leaks   ▶**Escape the Brain's Spam Filter**

274

Guess what? That's it.

We finally have our formula.

Improving our chances of making a sustainable bestselling product or service

Oh, and one last thing...

The Challenge   What Experts Do   Help Them Move Forward   **Support Cognitive Resources**
▼
Design   ▶Reduce Cognitive Leaks   ▶**Escape the Brain's Spam Filter**

276

Epilogue

Remember this from the beginning of the book?

Joining the engagement arms race with your competitors is not just fragile and tiring for *you*, it drains the limited cognitive resources of your *users*—resources they could use for something more meaningful to *them*.

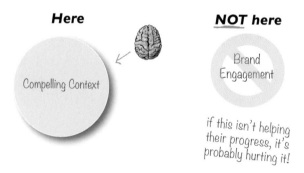

How much do we <u>really</u> care about our users?

Typical "brand engagement" strategy:

"Engaging with the Brand"

Working on becoming badass
(learning, practicing, experimenting, etc.)

good for BRAND

good for USERS

That one helpful YouTube video

Badass Users "brand engagement" strategy:

Working on becoming badass
(learning, practicing, experimenting, etc.)

"Engaging with the Brand"

good for
BRAND and
USERS

ALL our YouTube videos, blog posts,
"community" discussions, social
media interaction, live meet-ups,
sponsored activities.

> But what if our "brand engagement" is **fun?** What if it's a contest, or a game, or entertaining video? What if they **like** engaging with us on social media?

Don't make me explain "scarce, limited, zero-sum" again.

You can't have it both ways.

You can't entice users into spending time "engaging with your brand" *and* assume they'll use the *rest* of their time on learning, practice, and getting better.

Scare. Limited. Resources.

There's an exception, of course, and it's a crucial one: *if* you define "engaging with the brand" as *"actively involved in things we provide that make them better at the meaningful context they care about"*, then it's potentially useful. But that's not what most "brand engagement" is about.

Now take it a step further.

What *else* could our users be doing with the cognitive resources they spend "engaging with the brand"?

What *else* do they lose when we entice them into spending their time and cognitive resources interacting with our brand "content" or social media?

It's not just about saving their resources so they'll have more to spend on using (and getting better at) our product, or even the more meaningful bigger context.

If we *really* care about our users, we'll help them do what *they* want, not what *we* want.

If we *really* care about our users, we'll recognize that their goal in life is not simply to become badass at what *we* help them do, but to become...

Badass at life

You have the chance to help people become more skillful, more knowledgeable, more capable.

You have the chance to help make the world a little more high-res.

You have the chance to help people become better learners and better managers of their own limited cognitive resources.

You have the chance to help people spend more of their scarce, precious cognitive resources on the people they care about. (And don't forget the dog.)

You have the chance to raise the bar on what it means to care about users as *people* with lives. Complicated, *resource-draining* lives.

You have the chance to help people become more badass not only at using your tool within a meaningful context, but badass at *life*.

For all who made it this far, *thank-you* for using some of *your* scarce cognitive resources

I could use a few more of those resources right about now...

Yes, yes you could.

You need cognitive resources to help create badass users. So we'll leave you with a superpower of your own. A superpower you can draw on whenever you need it to *instantly* boost confidence, reduce stress, anxiety, and fear, increase pain tolerance, feel more optimistic, and more. In other words, an Instantly More Badass superpower.

It's not a self-help "positive thinking" mantra. It's science.

The science of Power Pose...

Power pose: *instant badass*

Instant badass

Adopting "high-power" posture has an instant effect on blood chemistry in a way that increases confidence and lowers stress. In two minutes!

More confidence + less stress = better learning/performance

Powererful postures don't just *reflect* power, they *create* it.

In 2012, researchers Amy Cuddy and Caroline Wilmuth at Harvard, and Dana Carney at Berkeley published a paper titled, "The Benefit of Power Posing *Before* a High-Stakes Social Evaluation." The experiment found that participants who adopted a "high-power" pose *before* preparing and delivering a speech to two evaluators in a mock job interview "performed better and were more likely to be chosen for hire."

But here's the jaw-dropping part: whether they were chosen for hire had nothing to do with candidate's posture *during* the interview. It was about the impact the power pose had on the their *preparation* for the interview.

In other words, the power pose exercise helped their chances for getting hired by changing what they did *before* they went in.

Power pose: *instant badass*

Instant badass

Amy Cuddy's TED talk.

You should watch it.

You should get your users to watch it too.

A few minutes of power posing can have a dramatic *instant* impact on our ability and willingness to keep moving forward when things get difficult or we're low on cognitive resources. In less that two minutes, holding a "power pose" (open, expansive, arms wide, think: superman or wonderwoman stance,) increases testosterone and lowers cortisol. Yes, less than two minutes.

Think about this. Whether your domain is programming, business modeling, or kung-fu, a well-timed power pose could be the crucial difference for someone on the verge of giving up. *Tell your users about it.*

"Don't fake it till you make it... fake it so you <u>become</u> it."
—Amy Cuddy

And now you're ready.

The end.

Acknowledgements

Long ago, Tim O'Reilly heard me talk about these ideas and said, "This should be a book." He got me *started*. But without Mark Littlewood, Stephen Kellet, Mike Brown, Natasha Lampard, Brian Bailey, Steinar Sigurbjörnsson, John Dodds, and Amy Hoy, I would never have *finished* it. They know why. You all have my heart.

Some of the amazing people I've learned from on my Badass Users journey include (in no particular order): Amy Jo Kim, Sebastian Deterding, Joel Spolsky, Jeff Atwood, Kevin Werbach, Mack Collier, Julie Dirksen, Clark Quinn, Thor Muller, Chad Fowler, Alex Hillman, Peter Morville, Andrew Hyde, Erin Kissane, Kristina Halvorson, Liza Sperling, Austin Kleon, Christina Wodtke, Hugh MacLeod, Chris Atherton, Matt Mullenweg, Jane Bozarth, Martin Fowler, Mark Hedlund, Redgate (yes, all of you), Simon Cast, Thomas Fuchs, Amy J. Cuddy, Jec Ballou, the folks at 37signals (especially Jason Fried and David Heinemeier Hansson), my kick-ass friends from O'Reilly— Mike Loukides, Courtney Nash, Meghan Blanchette, and Laura Baldwin, and the inspiring participants at Webstock NZ, Mind the Product, and Business of Software.

A bunch of smart, wonderful people helped me out on an early version of this book, including: Kip Hampton, Amrita Chandra, Justin Akehurst, Matt Jaynes, Alec Resnick, Noah Iliinsky, M Edward Borasky, and Ian Tyrrell.

Bert Bates knows more about deliberate practice than anyone I've ever met. Besides helping me develop the expertise chapters, he's been working with me on all parts of Badass over the last ten years.

I'm also thankful for all my online friends and supporters that did more for me than they can imagine, and with whom I shared my beautiful horses. This list is far from complete, but I'm going from memory here: @darth, @ericnormand, @johanjortso, @aurynn, @sammikes, @rivenhomewood, @lemay, @ignifluous, @waterprinciple, @mikecane, @cwodtke, @jwisser, @bug_gwen, @John_PeakApps, @dpatil, @fakebaldur, @brianwisti, @wndxlori, @iroc, @knowtheory, @stokely, @andrewjgrimm, @glv, @alexbaldwin, @sarahjbray, @chuq, @dshaw, @betsythemuffin, @grayj_, and @smd.

I'm forever grateful to those who helped me through a rough time while I finished this book: Anil Dash, Sarah Winge, Kevin Marks, Leigh Honeywell, Tim Bray, Faruk Ates, Tim Carmody, Danielle Citron, Elisabeth Robson, and Sarah Milstein.

Finally, I'm lucky to have a creative, inspiring, wild family including my exceptionally badass daughters Skyler and Eden, my sister Sherry who is *always* there, and the crew of smart, furry creatures I can't imagine life without.